ITALIAN SPANISH FRENCH
KEY WORDS

3 BOOKS IN ONE

Containing our 3 most popular language-learning titles - Spanish Key Words, Italian Key Words and French Key Words.

OLEANDER PRESS

THE OLEANDER PRESS
16 Orchard Street
Cambridge
CB1 1JT

www.oleanderpress.com

ISBN 9781999900410

CONTENTS

ITALIAN KEY WORDS

The basic 2,000-word vocabulary
arranged by frequency in a
hundred units.

With comprehensive Italian and
English indexes.

GIANPAOLO INTRONATI

The Oleander Press

The Oleander Press
16 Orchard Street
Cambridge
CB1 1JT

CONTENTS

Introduction

Italian Key Words provides an easy route to mastering excellent basic Italian. The 100-unit structure provides you with the most useful words quickly and easily, each unit consisting of 20 common words. These are the essential foundation stones on which you intuitively build your language framework. Computer analysis of a corpus of a million words has provided this essential list of the commonest two thousand key words in Italian, with their meanings in English, arranged in decreasing order of frequency.

The first five units (100 words) account for 50% of conversational Italian; the first 500 words account for 75% of normal usage; the full 2,000 will equip you for nearly all word occurrences of modern Italian usage in speech, newspapers, books, television, internet etc. It also provides an all-in-one basic Italian-English dictionary and an all-in-one basic English-Italian dictionary.

Italian Key Words is the perfect fast, easy aid to learning Italian by using the simplest, most logical way to pick up a vocabulary of ten thousand words from just two thousand.

The Units

Each of the one hundred units is deliberately self-contained for ease of mastery. Unit 1 contains the twenty commonest Italian words. Unit 2, the next twenty commonest and so on. The key word is followed by an indication of its part of speech: *adj*, adjective; *adv,* adverb; *conj*, conjunction; *f.n.*, feminine noun; *m.n.*, masculine noun; *prep*, preposition; *pron*, pronoun. Verbs are always represented by the infinitive, which in every case is translated by the commonest meanings beginning with 'to'.

Masculine nouns and adjectives form their feminine by changing o to a unless otherwise shown. So masculine *ricco* becomes *ricca*. Singular nouns and adjectives if masculine form their plural by changing o to i unless otherwise shown. So singular *povero* becomes plural poveri. Similarly, if feminine, singular nouns and adjectives form their plural by changing a to e unless otherwise shown. So singular *povera* becomes plural *povere*. *Lo stato povero* in the singular becomes *gli stati poveri* in the plural; and *la casa povera* becomes *le case povere.* (The change above in the article occurs because of the rule changing *il* to *lo* and *i* to *gli* before *gn, z,* and the so-called 'impure *s*', which refers to any *s* followed by a consonant, as in *lo sport.*)

Regular verbs are conjugated in the present tense in model form in a separate table. The commonest irregular verbs are conjugated in the present tense (of the active voice, indicative mood) wherever their infinitive occurs in the order of frequency. Though verbs appear only in their infinitive form, their position in the units is judged from the total occurrence of all their parts. Occasionally a phrase connected with a word, usually a verb, has been inserted where the phrase is particularly common or could not be constructed without special knowledge.

Many Italian words may be translated by a number of English equivalents. It would be counter-productive, in a work designed to stimulate interest rather than clog the memory, to list all such equivalents, so only the most common have been cited. When consulting the indexes, therefore, you should try to think of synonyms or near-synonyms if a given word appears not to be included.

These two indexes let the reader use *Italian Key Words* as a basic dictionary, but it should be stressed that the best full dictionary should be consulted if it is intended to continue with Italian past the elementary stage.

Regular Verbs in The Present Tense

First Conjugation   Parlare, to speak

io parlo	I speak	noi parliamo	we speak
tu parli	you speak	voi parlate	you (pl.) speak
lui, lei parla	he, she speaks	loro parlano	they speak

Second Conjugation   Temere, to fear

io temo	I fear	noi temiamo	we fear
tu temi	you fear	voi temete	you (pl.) fear
lui, lei teme	he, she fears	loro temono	they fear

Third Conjugation (Group 1)   Sentire, to feel, listen

io sento	I feel	noi sentiamo	we feel
tu senti	you feel	voi sentite	you (pl.) feel
lui, lei sente	he, she feels	loro sentono	they feel

Third Conjugation (Group2)* Capire, to understand

io capisco	I understand	noi capiamo	we understand
tu capisci	you understand	voi capite	you (pl.) understand
lui, lei capisce	he, she understands	loro capiscono	they understand

*Most 3rd conjugation verbs belong to this group, with the infix – isc – between stem and ending of the three singular persons and third person plural of the present, subjunctive and imperative.

di *prep.* — of
il *art.* — the *(m.s.)*
la *art.* — the *(f.s.)*
e *conj.* — and
a *prep.* — to
in *prep.* — in
uno, una *art.* — a, an *(m.,f.)*
essere — to be, being
   io sono — I am
   tu sei — you *(s.)* are
   lui è — he is
   noi siamo — we are
   voi siete — you *(pl.)* are
   loro sono — they are
lo *art.* — the *(m.s.)*, used instead of *il* before *gn*, impure *s* and *z*

che *pron.* — who, that
da *prep.* — from, by
per *prep.* — by, through
si *pron.* — one, –self
non *adv.* — not
con *prep.* — with
che *conj.* — than, that
avere — to have, having
   io ho — I have
   tu hai — you *(s.)* have
   lui ha — he has
   noi abbiamo — we have
   voi avete — you *(pl.)* have
   loro hanno — they have
questo, questa *adj.* — this

ma *conj.* — but
su *prep.* — on
lo *pron.* — him, it
potere — can, to be able
   io posso — I can   noi possiamo — we can
   tu puoi — you (*s.*) can   voi potete — you (*pl.*) can
   lui può — he can   loro possono — they can
o *conj.* — or
anche *adv.* — also, too
fare — to do, make
   io faccio — I do   noi facciamo — we do
   tu fai — you (*s.*) do   voi fate — you (*pl.*) do
   lui fa — he does   loro fanno — they do
quello, quella *adj.* — that
suo, sua *adj.* — his, her(s), its
tutto, tutta *adj.* — every, all
come *adv.* — as, like
più *adv.* — more
dire — to say
   io dico — I say   noi diciamo — we say
   tu dici — you (*s.*) say   voi dite — you (*pl.*) say
   lui dice — he says   loro dicono — they say
dovere — must, to have to
   io devo — I must   noi dobbiamo — we must
   tu devi — you (s.) must   voi dovete — you (*pl.*) must
   lui deve — he must   loro devono — they must
su *prep.* — on, upon
grande *adj.* — large, great
la *pron.* — her, it

stare — to stay, to remain
  io sto — I stay   noi stiamo — we stay
  tu stai — you (*s.*) stay   voi state — you (*pl.*) stay
  lui sta — he stays   loro stanno — they stay

ne *pron.* — some; of him, her, it (ne parlò con noi, he spoke of it with us)

quale *pron.* — which
due *num.* — two
venire — to come
  io vengo — I come   noi veniamo — we come
  tu vieni — you (*s.*) come   voi venite — you (*pl.*) come
  lui viene — he comes   loro vengono — they come

ci *pron.* — us, of it, to it, (eccoci qua, here we are)

altro, altra *adj.* — other
più *m.n. adj* — more
vedere — to see
  io vedo — I see   noi vediamo — we see
  tu vedi — you (*s.*) see   voi vedete — you (*pl.*) see
  egli vede — he sees   loro vedono — they see

quello, quella *pron.* — that one
ogni *adj.* — every, all
anno *m.n.* — year
perché *conj.* — why, because
volere — to want, to like
  io voglio — I want   noi vogliamo — we want
  tu vuoi — you (s.) want   voi volete — you (*pl.*) want
  lui vuole — he wants   loro vogliono — they want

mio, mia *adj.* — my
senza *prep.* — without
loro *adj.*, pron. — their, they

sempre *adv.*	always, still
nostro *adj.*	our, ours
ancora *adv.*	still, yet
così *adv.*	thus, so
se *conj.*	if, whether
giorno *m.n.*	day
come *prep.*	as, like
primo *adj.*	first
poi *adv.*	then, after(wards)
cui *pron.*	whom, which
trovare	to find
quando *conj.*	when
andare	to go

io vado	I go	noi andiamo	we go
tu vai	you go	voi andate	you go
lui va	he goes	loro vanno	they go

sapere — to know

io so	I know	noi sappiamo	we know
tu sai	you know	voi sapete	you know
lui sa	he knows	loro sanno	they know

io *pron.*	I
uomo *(pl.* uomini*) m.n.*	man
già	already, formerly, indeed
cosa *f.n.*	thing
parte *f.n.*	part
volta *f.n.*	time, turn

ora *adv.*	now
tra *prep.*	between, among
fra *prep.*	within, among
altro *pron.*	other
qualche *adj.*	some, a few (with *sing. n. e.g.* qualche minuto, some minutes)
nuovo *adj.*	new
vita *f.n.*	life
mi *pron.*	me, to me
egli *pron.*	he
lui *pron.*	he, him
ora *f.n.*	hour, time
dove *adj.*	where
parlare	to speak
dopo *prep.*	after(wards)
noi *pron.*	we
tempo *m.n.*	time, whether
sembrare	to seem, look

io sembro	I appear	noi sembriamo	we appear
tu sembri	you appear	voi sembrate	you appear
lui sembra	he appears	loro sembrano	they appear

modo *m.n.*	way, manner(s)
prendere	to take, catch

io prendo	I take	noi prendiamo	we take
tu prendi	you take	voi prendete	you take
lui prende	he takes	loro prendono	they take

passare	to pass
le *pron.*	to her, them
portare	to carry, wear
uno *pron.*	one
sè *pron.*	himself, herself, *etc.*
stesso *adj.*	same, self
pure *adv.*	yet, likewise
questo,questa *pron.*	this
sotto *prep.*	below, under
mettere	to put, place

io metto	I put	noi mettiamo	we put
tu metti	you put	voi mettete	you put
lui mette	he puts	loro mettono	they put

solamente *adv.*	only
li *pron.*	them
casa *f.n.*	house
bello *adj.*	handsome, beautiful
lasciare	to let, allow
forse *adv.*	perhaps, maybe
allora *adv.*	then
esso,essa *pron.*	he, she, it

parola *f.n.* — word
piccolo *adj.* — small
vero *adj.* — real, true
chi *pron.* — who(ever), whom
ti *pron.* — you (*s.*)
buono *adj.* — good
mai *adv.* — (n)ever
molto *adj.* — very, much
tenere — to keep, hold
   io tengo — I keep   noi teniamo — we keep
   tu tieni — you keep   voi tenete — you keep
   lui tiene — he keeps   loro tengono — they keep
solo *adj* — alone, only
certo *adj* — sure, certain
lavoro *m.n.* — work, job
tre *num.* — three
pensare — to think
poco *adj* — little, few
sembrare — to seem, appear
ultimo *adj* — last
bene *adv.* — well
alcuno *adj.* — some, any
rimanere — to stay, to remain
   io rimango — I stay   noi remaniamo — we stay
   tu rimani — you stay   voi rimanete — you stay
   lui rimane — he stays   loro rimangono — they stay

Unit 8

donna *f.n.*	lady, woman
qui *adv.*	here
nome *m.n.*	name, noun
vi *pron.*	you, to you
contro *prep.*	against
alto *adj.*	high, tall
occhio *m.n.*	eye
oggi *adv.*	today
chiamare	to call,
via *f.n.*	way, street
né *conj.*	neither, nor
mano (*pl.* le mani) *f.n.*	hand
guardare	to look at, keep
mondo *m.n.*	world
proprio *adj.*	proper, neat
vecchio *adj.*	old
punto *m.n.*	point
città *f.n*	city
ciò *pron.*	that, this, it
credere	to believe

momento *m.n.* — moment
prima *adv.* — before, earlier
terra *f.n.* — land, earth
tale *adj.* — such, like
subito *adv.* — suddenly
quasi *adv.* — almost, as if
tanto *adj.* — so much, such
verso *prep.* — towards
mentre *conj.* — while, whereas
fatto *m.n.* — fact, act(ion)
loro *pron.* — they
arrivare — to arrive, reach

io arrivo	I arrive	noi arriviamo	we arrive
tu arrivi	you arrive	voi arrivate	you arrive
lui arriva	he arrives	loro arrivano	they arrive

cercare *num.* — to seek, try
Italiano *adj.* — Italian
nulla *adv.* — nothing
me *pron.* — me
padre *m.n.* — father
guerra *f.n.* — war
uscire — to go out

io esco	I go out	noi usciamo	we go out
tu esci	you go out	voi uscite	you go out
lui esce	he goes out	loro escono	they go out

mare *m.n.* — sea

conoscere — to know
  io conosco — I know
  tu conosci — you know
  egli conosce — he knows
  noi conosciamo — we know
  voi conoscete — you know
  loro conoscono — they know

però *conj.* — however, but
tornare — to return
acqua *f.n.* — water
entrare — to enter
forza *f.n.* — strength, power
notte *f.n.* — night
amore *m.n.* — love
figlio *m.n.* — son, boy
luce *f.n.* — light
cuore *m.n.* — heart
invece *adv.* — instead, on the contrary
caso *m.n.* — case, event

vivere — to live
  io vivo — I live
  tu vivi — you live
  lui vive — he lives
  noi viviamo — we live
  voi vivite — you live
  loro vivono — they live

anzi *adv.* — rather, on the contrary
cominciare — to begin
là *adv.* — there

sentire — to feel, listen
  io sento — I feel
  tu senti — you feel
  lui sente — he feels
  noi sentiamo — we feel
  voi sentite — you feel
  loro sentono — they feel

opera *f.n.* — work, opera

riuscire — to succeed, to come out
  io riesco — I succeed
  tu riesci — you succeed
  lui riesce — he succeeds
  noi riusciamo — we succeed
  voi riuscite — you succeed
  loro riescono — they succeed

aria *f.n.* — air, breeze

lei *pron.* — she, her

seguire — to follow (conjugated like sentire)

sopra *prep.* — upon, above

gente *f.n.* — people

rendere — to give back, yield, return

io rendo	I give back	noi rendiamo	we give back
tu rendi	you give back	voi rendete	you give back
lui rende	he gives back	loro rendono	they give back

capo *m.n.* — Head, chief

apparire — to appear

io appaio	I appear	noi appariamo	we appear
tu appari	you appear	voi apparite	you appear
lui appare	he appears	loro appaiono	they appear

luogo *m.n.* — place

scrivere — to write

io scrivo	I write	noi scriviamo	we write
tu scrivi	you write	voi scrivete	you write
lui scrive	he writes	loro scrivono	they write

paese *m.n.* — land, town, village

presentare — to present

maggiore *adj.* — greater, elder

aver bisogno di — to need, be necessary (bisogna scrivere, one must write)

continuare — to continue

aprire — to open

io apro	I open	noi apriamo	we open
tu apri	you open	voi aprite	you open
lui apre	he opens	loro aprono	they open

pensiero *m.n.* — thought

ordine *m.n.* — order, command

diventare — to become

idea *f.n.* — idea

riconoscere		to recognise (conjugated like conoscere)	
fino *prep.*		until, as long as	
servire		to serve (conjugated like sentire)	
rappresentare		to represent, perform	
intorno *prep.*		around	
diverso *adj.*		different, various	
chidere		to ask	
io chiedo	I ask	noi chiediamo	we ask
tu chiedi	you ask	voi chiedete	you ask
lui chiede	he asks	loro chiedono	they ask
madre *f.n.*		mother	
quattro *num.*		four	
mese *m.n.*		month	
popolo *m.n.*		people	
cioè *adv.*		that is	
anima *f.n.*		soul	
pieno *adj.*		full	
morte *f.n.*		death	
secondo *adj.*		second, next	
sera *f.n.*		evening	
quindi *adv.*		therefore, afterwards	
famiglia *f.n.*		family	

voce *f.n.*
voice

restare
to stay, remain

fondo *m.n.*
end, background, bottom

morire
to die

   io muoio — I die
   tu muori — you die
   lui muore — he dies
   noi moriamo — we die
   voi morite — you die
   loro muoiono — they die

durante *prep.*
during

camera *f.n.*
room, chamber (*Eng.* Camera is *It.* macchina fotografica)

correre
to run

   io corro — I run
   tu corri — you run
   lui corre — he run
   noi corriamo — we run
   voi correte — you run
   loro corrono — they run

sole *m.n.*
sun

comprendere
to understand, include (conjugated like prendere)

nascere
to be born

   io nasco — I am born
   tu nasci — you are born
   lui nasce — he is born
   noi nasciamo — we are born
   voi nascete — you are born
   loro nascono — they are born

quale *adj.*
which, who

dunque *adv.*
so, then

trattare
to deal with, handle

presso *prep.*
near, by

corpo *m.n.*
body

arrivare
to arrive

ragione *f.n.*
reason, right (aver ragione, to be right)

vivo *adj.*
living

partire
to depart, set out (conjugated like sentire)

esistere
to exist

   io esisto — I exist
   tu estiti — you exist
   lui esiste — he exists
   noi esistiamo — we exist
   voi esistete — you exist
   loro esitono — they exist

antico *adj.*		ancient, old	
condurre		to lead	
io conduco	I lead	noi conduciamo	we lead
tu conduci	you lead	voi conducete	you lead
lui conduce	he leads	loro conducono	they lead
mostrare		to show	
libro *m.n.*		book	
professore *m.n.*		professor, teacher	
chiudere		to close	
io chiudo	I close	noi chiudiamo	we close
tu chiudi	you close	voi chiudete	you close
lui chiude	he closes	loro chiudono	they close
vario *adj.*		various, different	
insieme *adv.*		together	
persona *f.n.*		person	
valore *m.n.*		value, courage	
cielo *m.n.*		sky, heaven	
campo *m.n.*		field, camp	
stato *m.n.*		state	
lungo *adj.*		long, tall	
aspettarc		to wait, expect	
nessuno *pron.*		nobody, none	
intendere		to mean, understand (conjugated like prendere)	
strada *f.n.*		street, way	
finire		to finish (conjugated like capire)	
chiaro *adj.*		clear, bright	

salire
   io salgo
   tu sali
   lui sale
appena *adv.*
cadere
   io cado
   tu cadi
   lui cade
carattere *m.n.*
possible *adj.*
perdere
   io perdo
   tu perdi
   lui perde
generale *adj.*
amico *m.n.*
compiere
   io compio
   tu compi
   lui compie
figura *f.n.*
spirito *m.n.*
azione *f.n.*

lontano *adj.*
umano *adj.*
no *adv.*

to climb, go up
   noi saliamo
   voi salite
   loro salgono
only, as soon as
to fall, drop
   noi cadiamo
   voi cadete
   loro cadono
character
possible
to lose
   noi perdiamo
   voi perdete
   loro perdono
general
friend
to complete, finish
   noi compiamo
   voi compite
   loro compiono
figure
spirit, wit
action (but It. azione ordinaria in commerce is Eng. ordinary share)
far, distant
human
no

rispondere	to respond, answer
io rispondo	noi rispondiamo
tu rispondi	voi rispondete
lui risponde	loro rispondono
mancare	to lack, miss
io manco	noi manchiamo
tu manchi	voi mancate
egli manca	loro mancano
signore *m.n.*	sir, Mr, gentleman
capire	to understand
io capisco	noi capiamo
tu capisci	voi capite
lui capisce	loro capiscono
esempio *m.n.*	example
testa *f.n.*	head
ricco *adj.*	rich
ormai *adv.*	by now, henceforth
raggiungere	to achieve, reach
io raggiungo	noi raggiungiamo
tu raggiungi	voi raggiungete
lui raggiunge	loro raggiungono
second *adj.*	second, next
chiesa *f.n.*	church
arte *f.n.*	art
accompagnare	to accompany
lettera *f.n.*	letter
grave *adj.*	heavy, serious
quanto *adv.*	how, how much
conto *m.n.*	account
almeno *conj.*	at least
secolo *m.n.*	century

problema *m.n.* (pl. problemi)	problem
leggere	to read
io leggo	noi leggiamo
tu leggi	voi leggete
lui legge	loro leggono
piede *m.n.*	foot
specie *f.n.*	species, kind
marito *m.n.*	husband
meglio *adv.*	better
troppo *adj.*	too much
studio *m.n.*	study
diritto *m.n.*	right, law
necessario *adj.*	necessary
bastare	to suffice, be enough
resto *m.n.*	rest, change
attraverso *prep.*	across, through
lì *adv.*	there
avvenire	to happen (conjugated like venire)
governo *m.n.*	government, control
raccogliere	to collect together, gather in
io raccolgo	noi raccogliamo
tu raccogli	voi raccogliete
lui raccoglie	loro raccolgono
spesso *adv.*	often
forma *f.n.*	form
sangue *m.n.*	blood

nessuno *adj.*	nobody
forte *adj.*	strong
specialmente *adv.*	especially
palazzo *m.n.*	palace
amare	to love
legge *f.n.*	law
infatti *adv.*	in fact
semplice *adj.*	simple
voi *pron.*	you (*pl.*)
viaggio *m.n.*	journey
verità *f.n.* (*pl.* verità)	truth
perché *conj.*	because, why
dimostrare	to show
tu *pron.*	you (*s.*)
braccio *m.n.s.* (*pl.* is *f,*: le braccia)	arm
felice *adj.*	happy
meno *adj.*	less
scuola *f.n.*	school

giovane *adj.*	young
faccia *f.n.*	face
comune *adj.*	common
ripetere	to repeat (conjugated like temere)
signora *f.n.*	Madam, Mrs, lady
importanza *f.n.*	importance
interesse *m.n.*	interest
oro *m.n.*	gold
permettere	to allow, permit (conjugated like mettere)
numero *m.n.*	number
politico *adj.*	political
fermare	to stop, fix
incontrare	to meet
vostro *adj.*	your
costituire	to constitute (conjugated like capire)
colore *m.n.*	colour
bisogno *m.n.*	need
quasi *adj.*	almost
notare	to note
ritornare	to return

tuo *adj.*	your
circa *adv.*	about, roughly
notizia *f.n.*	notice, news
moglie *f.n.*	wife
considerare	to consider
veramente *adv.*	really
preparare	to prepare
mentre *m.n.*	while (in quel mentre, in the moment)
paura *f.n.*	fear
discorso *m.n.*	speech, lecture
libero *adj.*	free
linea *f.n.*	line
profondo *adj.*	deep
tanto *adv.*	so, so much
gruppo *m.n.*	group
fino *adv.*	until, as long as
valere	to count, be worth
io valgo	noi valiamo
tu vali	voi valete
lui vale	loro valgono
nazionale *adj.*	national
osservare	to observe
durare	to last

sicuro *adj.*	sure, steady
società *f.n.* (*pl.* Società)	society
nero *adj.*	black
natura *f.n.*	nature
tutto *adv.*	all, very
giornata *f.n.*	day
te *pron.*	you, to you (*s.*) (te l'ho promesso, I promised it to you)
genere *m.n.*	kind, genus
breve *adj.*	brief, short
colpo *m.n.*	blow, kick
quanto *pron.*	how much
posto *m.n.*	place
unico *adj.*	only
fortuna *f.n.*	fortune, luck
domandare	to ask
sala *f.n.*	hall, room
mezzo *m.n.*	half,
istituto *m.n.*	institute
trarre	to drag, pull
io traggo	noi traiamo
tu trai	voi traete
lui trae	loro traggono

posare — to lay, set down
atto *m.n.* — act
perciò *adv.* — therefore
offrire — to offer
   io offro — noi offriamo
   tu offri — voi offrite
   lui offre — loro offrono
dottore *m.n.* (*f.* dottoressa) — doctor (medical, academic)
autore *m.n.* (*f.* autrice) — author
misura *f.n.* — measure(ment)
recevere — to receive (conjugated like temere)

aspetto *m.n.* — appearance, (sala d'aspetto, waiting room)

età *f.n.* (*pl.* età) — age, epoch
fuori *adv.* — outside
via *adv.* — away (andare via, to go away)
toccare — to touch
tentare — to attempt, tempt
vista *f.n.* — view, sight
muro *m.n.* (*pl.* muri or mura) — wall
mandare — to send
meno *adv.* — less, least
necessità *f.n.* (*pl.* necessità) — need
potenza *f.n.* — power

controllo *m.n.*	control
aperto *adj.*	open
element *m.n.*	element
prima *adv.*	before
caro *adj.*	dear
occupare	to occupy
presente *adj.*	present
ascoltare	to listen
occorrere	need (non mi occorre nient' altro, I don't need anything else) conjugated like correre
natural *adj.*	Natural
largo *adj.*	Wide
fronte *m.n.*	front, brow
formare	to form, instruct
avvertire	to warn, inform (conjugated like sentire)
grosso *adj.*	fat, thick
numeroso *adj.*	numerous
creare	to create
ecco *adv.*	(t)here is, are (ecco! look!)
tavolo *f.n.*	table
simile *adj.*	similar, such
posizione *f.n.*	position
lavorare	to work

grazia *f.n.* — grace, charm (grazie, thanks)

automobile *f.n.* — motor-car (generally replaced colloquially by 'macchina')

porre — to put, place
  io pongo — noi poniamo
  tu poni — voi ponete
  lui pone — loro pongono

moderno *adj.* — modern

rapporto *m.n.* — report, relation

tratto *m.n.* — Stroke, line

ci *adv.* (ce *with* ne) — here, there (non ce ne sono più, there are none left)

possibilità *f.n.* (*pl.* possibilità) — possibility

onore *m.n.* — honour

volontà *f.n.* (*pl.* volontà) — will

proporre — to propose (conjugated like porre)

corso *m.n.* — course, currency

muovere — to move
  io muovo — noi moviamo
  tu muovi — voi movete
  lui muove — loro muovono

basso *adj.* — low

ricordo *m.n.* — memory, souvenir

fede *f.n.* — faith

bianco *adj.* — white, blank

bocca *f.n.* — mouth

davanti *prep.* — in front

consiglio *m.n.* — council, advice

morto *adj.*	dead
attendere	to attend to, wait for (conjugated like prendere)
particolare *adj.*	particular
fratello *m.n.*	brother
ridere	to laugh
io rido	noi ridiamo
tu ridi	voi ridete
lui ride	loro ridono
straordinario *adj.*	extraordinary
scopo *m.n.*	purpose
periodo *m.n.*	period
bambino *m.n.*	child
metà *f.n.*	half
giovane adj, *m.n*	young
dieci *num.*	ten
riprendere	to regain, resume (conjugated like prendere)
fine *f.n.*	end
lei *pron.*	she
espressione *f.n.*	expression
passione *f.n.*	passion
fuoco *m.n.*	fire
servizio *m.n.*	service
romano *adj.*	Roman

effetto *m.n.*	effect
dietro *prep.*	behind
aggiungere	to add (conjugated like raggiungere)
superiore *adj.*	superior, higher
cinque *num.*	five
giro *m.n.*	turn, stroll
mezzo *adj.*	middle, half
giù *adv.*	down(wards)
ottenere	to obtain (conjugated like tenere)
proprio *m.n.*	one's own
scena *f.n.*	scene, stage
sentire (a sound)	to hear
io sento	noi sentiamo
tu senti	voi sentite
lui sente	loro sentono
caldo *adj.*	hot
scendere	to go down, alight (conjugated like prendere)
fermo *adj.*	steady, firm
argomento *m.n.*	argument, subject
molto *adv.*	very, much
festa *f.n.*	festival, holiday
accordo *m.n.*	agreement
massimo *adj.*	greatest, supreme
mattina *f.n.*	morning

mantenere	to maintain, hold (conjugated like tenere)
stazione *f.n.*	Station
pubblicare	to publish
bene *m.n.*	good
dimenticare	to forget
riferire	to refer (conjugated like capire)
dubbio *m.n.*	doubt
porta *f.n.*	door, gate
funzione *f.n.*	function
davvero *adv.*	really
migliore *adj.*	better (il migliore, the best)
accettare	to accept
assai *adv.*	very much, enough
lingua *f.n.*	tongue, language
fiore *m.n.*	flower
svolgere	to develop, unfold

io svolgo	noi svolgiamo
tu svolgi	voi svolgete
lui svolge	loro svolgono

vasto *adj.*	vast
memoria *f.n.*	memory
desiderio *m.n.*	desire
passo *m.n.*	step, passage

male *m.n.*	evil, illness
sistema *m.n.* (*pl.* i sistemi)	system
sentimento *m.n.*	feeling, sensibility
piacere	to like (mi piace, I like it)
io piaccio	noi piacciamo
tu piaci	voi piacete
lui piace	loro piacciono
speciale *adj.*	special
ufficio *m.n.*	office
due *pron.*	two (tutti e due, both)
chiuso *adj.*	closed
togliere	to take away, remove (conjugated like raccogliere)
sviluppo *m.n.*	development
tacere	to be silent (conjugated like piacere)
giardino *m.n.*	garden
riguardare	to concern, look at again
preciso *adj.*	precise
tardi *adv.*	late *but* il fu Mattia Pascal, the late Mattia Pascal)
cura *f.n.*	care
piazza *f.n.*	square
interessante *adj.*	interesting
giornale *m.n.*	journal, newspaper

oggetto *m.n.*	object
questione *f.n.*	question
poco *adv.*	few, little (fra poco, shortly)
sogno *m.n.*	dream
campagna *f.n.*	country(side), campaign
ritrovare	to recover, find again
assicurare	to assure, insure
relazione *f.n.*	report, relation
certamente *adv.*	certainly
pena *f.n.*	punishment, trouble
dolore *m.n.*	sorrow, pain
vicino *adj.*	near
facile *adj.*	easy
portare	to bring
carta *f.n.*	paper, card, map
santo *adj.*	holy
gioia *f.n.*	happiness, jewel
spiegare	to explain
assai *adj.*	very
giusto *adj.*	just, correct, accurate

difficile *adj.*	difficult
rosso *adj.*	red
divenire	to become (conjugated like venire)
pratico *adj.*	practical
nazione *f.n.*	nation
troppo *adv.*	too much
qua *adv.*	here
scoprire	to discover (conjugated like coprire)
impression *f.n.*	impression
studiare	to study
importante *adj.*	important
movimento *m.n.*	movement
silenzio *f.n.*	silence
esperienza *f.n.*	experience
lì *adv.*	there
ombra *f.n.*	shade
presto *adv.*	quickly, early
oltre *adv.*	beyond
principe *m.n.*	prince
spingere	to push

io spingo	noi spingiamo
tu spingi	voi spingete
lui spinge	loro spingono

usare	to use
intanto *adv.*	meanwhile
attività *f.n.* (*pl.* le attività)	activity
dovere *m.n*	duty
causa *f.n.*	cause
sorgere	to spring, rise
io sorgo	noi sorgiamo
tu sorgi	voi sorgete
lui sorge	loro sorgono
corrispondere	to correspond (conjugated like rispondere)
sottile *adj.*	thin, subtle
sperare	to hope
lira *f.n.*	lira (old currency)
villa *f.n.*	villa, country-house
recente *adj.*	recent
scienza *f.n.*	science
dentro *prep.*	within, inside
concedere	to allow
io concedo	noi concediamo
tu concedi	voi concedete
lui concede	loro concedono
storia *f.n.*	history
naturalmente *adv.*	naturally
nemico *m.n.*	enemy
disporre	to dispose, arrange (conjugated like porre)
fuori *prep.*	outside

realtà *f.n.* (*pl.* realtà)	reality
finestra *f.n.*	window
ragazzo *m.n.*	boy
fissare	to fix
prova *f.n.*	proof, examination
decidere	to decide (conjugated like ridere)
povero *adj.*	poor
mangiare	to eat
tuttavia *adv.*	still, nevertheless
presenza *f.n.*	presence
accanto *prep.*	near, beside
intero *adj.*	whole
proposito *m.n.*	intention, (a proposito! by the way!)
puro *adj.*	pure
impedire	to hinder (conjugated like capire)
dinanzi *prep.*	in front
primo *m.n.*	first
sacro *adj.*	holy
mente *f.n.*	mind

macchina *f.n.*	machine, motor-car
pubblico *m.n.*	public
esprimere	to express
io esprimo	noi esprimiamo
tu esprimi	voi esprimete
lui esprime	loro esprimono
albero *m.n.*	tree
peso *m.n.*	weight
concetto *m.n.*	concept
particolare *m.n.*	specific, detail
eccetera *m.n.* (no plural)	et cetera
alzare	to raise, lift
contenere	to contain (conjugated like tenere)
tipo *m.n.*	type, kind
termine *m.n.*	end, boundary
sedersi	to sit
io mi siedo	noi ci sediamo
tu ti siedi	voi vi sedete
lui si siede	loro si siedono
abbandonare	to abandon
triste *adj.*	sad
piuttosto *adv.*	rather
monte *m.n.*	mountain
sopratutto *adv.*	above all
ritorno *m.n.*	return
qualcuno *pron.*	someone, somebody

quanto *adj.*	how much, how many
rivolgere	to turn (over) (conjugated like svolgere)
seguente *adj.*	following
assumere	to accept, hire, raise
io assumo	noi assumiamo
tu assumi	voi assumete
lui assume	loro assumono
occasione *f.n.*	occasion
salutare	to greet
colui *pron.*	he, he who
letto *m.n.*	bed
dentro *adv.*	inside
difficoltà *f.n.* (*pl.* difficoltà)	difficulty
levare	to raise, remove
lato *m.n.*	side
affare *m.n.*	affair (uomo d'affari, businessman)
spalla *f.n.*	shoulder
nascondere	to hide (conjugated like rispondere)
minuto *m.n.*	minute
leggero *adj.*	light
stella *f.n.*	star
dividere	to divide (conjugated like ridere)
immaginare	to imagine

settimana *f.n.* — week
volto *m.n.* — face
dove *adv.* — where
libertà *f.n.* (*pl.* libertà) — freedom
finalmente *adv.* — finally
strano *adj.* — strange
neppure *adv.* — not even
dolce *adj.* — sweet
oh! *interj.* — oh!
dormire — to sleep (conjugated like sentire)
segnare — to mark, note
perfetto *adj.* — perfect
poeta *m.n.* (*f.n.* poetessa, poetesse) (*pl.* i poeti) — poet
fuggire — to flee (conjugated like sentire)
grado *m.n.* — degree, (di buon grado, willingly)
possedere — to possess (conjugated like sedere)
musica *f.n.* — music
principio *m.n.* — beginning, principle
mutare — to change
freddo *adj.* — cold

sostenere	to support, sustain (conjugated like tenere)
conoscenza *f.n.*	acquaintance
succedere	to happen
io succedo	noi succediamo
tu succedi	voi succedete
lui succede	loro succedono
pregare	to pray, ask
inglese *adj.*	English
sede *f.n.*	seat
inverno *m.n.*	winter
maestro *m.n.*	master, tutor
situazione *f.n.*	situation
ammettere	to admit (conjugated like mettere)
ferro *m.n.*	iron
interessare	to interest
mamma *f.n.*	mother, mama
terzo *adj.*	third
animale *m.n.*	animal
tendere	to stretch (out), spread (conjugated like prendere)
cantare	to sing
motivo *m.n.*	cause, theme
salvare	to save
pronto *adj.*	ready, quick (pronto! hello!)
attenzione *f.n.*	attention

pietà *f.n.* (*pl.* pieta)	pity
fiume *m.n.*	river
storico *adj.*	historic
infine *adv.*	finally
cavallo *m.n.*	horse
destino *m.n.*	fate, destiny
carne *f.n.*	meat, flesh
significato *m.n.*	meaning
nota *f.n.*	note
liberare	to relieve, liberate
tale *pron.*	such
accogliere	to receive, accept (conjugated like raccogliere)
verde *adj.*	green
economico *adj.*	cheap
soffrire	to suffer (conjugated like aprire)
maniera *f.n.*	manner, way
italiano *m.n.*	Italian
avvicinare	to approach
ministro *m.n.*	minister

conservare	to keep, preserve
stretto *adj.*	narrow, strict
sforzo *m.n.*	effort
direttore *m.n.*	director
viso *m.n.*	face
angolo	corner, angle
limitare	to limit
disposizione *f.n.*	disposition
cui *pron.*	whose
evitare	to avoid
fresco *adj.*	fresh, cool
delicato *adj.*	delicate
origine *f.n.*	origin
desiderare	to desire
oscuro *adj.*	dark
costruire	to build (conjugated like capire)
bere	to drink
io bevo	noi beviamo
tu bevi	voi bevete
lui beve	bevono
volume *m.n.*	volume
successo *m.n.*	success, result
zona *f.n.*	zone

lotta *f.n.*	struggle
entro *prep.*	within
alto *m.n.*	height, top
ampio *adj.*	wide, ample
centro *m.n.*	centre
limite *m.n.*	limit, border
convenire	to suit, be convenient (conviene partire, it is better to leave) (conjugated like venire)
certo *adv.*	certainly
qualcosa *pron.*	something
industria *f.n.*	industry
appartenere	to belong to (conjugated like tenere)
religioso *adj.*	religious
ieri *adv.*	yesterday
iniziare	to begin
pietra *f.n.*	rock
imporre	to impose (conjugated like pore)
patria f.n.	native country
serio *adj.*	serious
circolo *m.n.*	circle
ponte *m.n.*	bridge

pagina *f.n.*	page
gioco *m.n.*	game, sport, play
cambiare	to (ex)change
immenso *adj.*	immense
vicino *adv.*	close by
discussion *f.n.*	discussion
provare	to try, test, experience, rehearse
uccidere	to kill (conjugated like ridere)
nemmeno *adv.*	not even
senso *m.n.*	sense, direction
temere	to fear (conjugated on Regular Verbs page)
artista *f., m.n.* (*pl.* artisti)	artist
università *f.n.* (*pl.* università)	university
immagine *f.n.*	image
stabilire	to establish (conjugated like capire)
notevole *adj.*	notable
offendere	to offend (conjugated like prendere)

speranza *f.n.*	hope
crescere	to grow
io cresco	noi cresciamo
tu cresci	voi crescete
lui cresce	loro crescono
frase *f.n.*	sentence, phrase
errore *m.n.*	error
pericolo *m.n.*	danger
ridurre	to reduce
io riduco	noi riduciamo
tu riduci	voi riducete
lui riduce	loro riducono
utile *adj.*	useful
uso *m.n.*	use
appunto *adv.*	precisely
niente *m.n.*	nothing
canto *m.n.*	song, side
noto *adj.*	known
scegliere	to choose
io scelgo	noi scegliamo
tu scegli	voi schgliete
lui sceglie	loro scelgono
politica *f.n.* (*pl.* politica)	politics
sociale *adj.*	social
principale *adj.*	principal
camminare	to walk, go
pubblico *adj.*	public
domanda *f.n.*	question
indurre	to lead, induce (conjugated like ridurre)

esporre — to expose, exhibit (conjugated like porre)

enorme *adj.* — enormous
terreno *m.n.* — site, ground
difendere — to defend (conjugated like prendere)

passato *m.n.* — past
abito *m.n.* — coat, dress, (monastic) habit
accorgersi — to notice, realize
ah! *interj.* — ah!
sguardo *m.n.* — look, glance
risolvere — to resolve
  io risolvo   noi resolviamo
  tu risolvi   voi risolvete
  lui risolve   loro risolvono
Ordinare — to order, arrange
estremo *adj.* — extreme
medesimo *adj.* — same
accennare — to indicate
raccontare — to tell
risultato *m.n.* — result
battere — to beat (conjugated like tenere)
grido *m.n.* — shout
esistenza *f.n.* — existence
distruggere — to destroy
  io distruggo   noi distruggiamo
  tu distruggi   voi distruggete
  lui distrugge   loro distruggono

teatro *m.n.*	theatre
legare	to bind
tanto *m.n.*	A lot
osservazione *f.n.*	Observation
costui *pron.*	that one (i.e. man)
stagione *f.n.*	season
classe *f.n.*	class
stanza *f.n.*	room
contare	to count, reckon
manifestare	to reveal, show
civiltà *f.n.* (*pl.* civiltà)	civilisation
coprire	to cover (conjugated like aprire)
attorno *prep.*	around
scala *f.n.*	ladder, scale
quadro *m.n.*	picture
albergo *m.n.*	hotel
improvviso *adj.*	sudden
ritenere	to retain, hold (back)(conjugated like tenere)
malattia *f.n.*	sickness
procedere	to proceed (conjugated like succedere)

continuo *adj.*	continuous
superare	to overcome (superare gli esami, to pass examinations)
concludere	to conclude (conjugated like chiudere)
inutile *adj.*	useless
preferire	to prefer (conjugated like capire)
collo *m.n.*	neck
produrre	to produce (conjugated like ridurre)
mediterraneo *adj.*	Mediterranean
frutto *m.n.*	fruit
umanità *f.n.* (*pl.* umanità)	humanity
riportare	to report, return, carry forward
intimo *adj.*	intimate
ramo *m.n.*	branch
soldato *m.n.*	soldier
indicare	to indicate
sereno *adj.*	sunny
sollevare	to lift, raise, comfort
vincere	to conquer, defeat, win

io vinco	noi vinciamo
tu vinci	voi vincete
lui vince	loro vincono

compagno *m.n.*	companion
rivelare	to reveal
primavera *f.n.*	spring
conseguenza *f.n.*	consequence
rapido *adj.*	quick
isola *f.n.*	island
virtù *f.n.* (*pl.* virtù)	virtue
spettacolo *m.n.*	show, performance
bellezza *f.n.*	beauty
comporre	to compose (conjugated like porre)
folla *f.n.*	crowd
baciare	to kiss
ognuno *pron.*	everyone
base *f.n.*	base, basis
uguale *adj.*	equal
luna *f.n.*	moon
creatura *f.n.*	creature
commedia *f.n.*	comedy

gusto *m.n.* — taste

piangere — to cry
  io piango / noi piangiamo
  tu piangi / voi piangete
  lui piange / loro piangono

affatto *adv.* — entirely (niente affatto, not at all)

parete *f.n.* — wall

fatica *f.n.* — fatigue, work, trouble

arma *f.n.* (*pl.* le armi) — weapon

insegnare — to teach

infinito *adj.* — infinite

provvedere — to provide (conjugated like vedere)

aiutare — to help

cattivo *adj.* — bad, naughty

signorina *f.n.* — Miss, young lady

illustre *adj.* — distinguished, famous

gettare — to throw

assoluto *adj.* — absolute

affermare — to assert, affirm

aiuto *m.n.* — help

qualità *f.n.* (*pl.* qualità) — quality

riflettere — to reflect
  io rifletto / noi riflettiamo
  tu rifletti / voi riflettete
  lui riflette / loro riflettono

adesso *adv.*	now
minore *adj.*	minor, less, smaller
allontanare	to remove, send away
giudicare	to judge
sorridere	to smile (conjugated like ridere)
padrone *m.n.*	master, owner
ottimo *adj.*	excellent, best
dirigere	to direct, lead
io dirigo	noi dirigiamo
tu dirigi	voi dirigete
lui dirige	loro dirigono
venti *num.*	twenty
filo *m.n.*	thread, wire
sorella *f.n.*	sister
osare	to dare
proprietà *f.n.* (*pl.* proprietà)	property
alcuno *pron.*	somebody, someone, no-one
richiamare	to recall, call back
maggio *m.n.*	May
brutto *m.n.*	ugly, bad, nasty
suono *m.n.*	sound
completamente *adv.*	completely

salute	*m.n.*	health
dichiarare		to declare
peccato	*m.n.*	sin, shame
attraversare		to cross
riudire		to hear again (conjugated like udire)
epoca	*f.n.*	epoch, period
singolare	*adj.*	singular
tagliare		to cut
riguardo	*m.n.*	regard, consideration
cristiano	*adj.*	Christian
cento	*num.*	hundred
confermare		to confirm
girare		to turn round, circulate
degno	*adj.*	worthy
accendere		to light (accendere la luce, put on the light) (conjugated like prendere)
assistere		to witness, aid (conjugated like esistere)
ricchezza	*f.n.*	wealth
tranquillo	adj.	quite
morale	*adj.*	moral
animo	*m.n.*	mind, courage

produzione *f.n.*	production
appoggiare	to lean, back up
giustizia *f.n.*	justice
importare	to import, be important (non importa, it doesn't matter)
fantasia *f.n.*	fancy, imagination
pagare	to pay
energia *f.n*	energy
nobile *adj.*	noble
colpa *f.n.*	fault, guilt, blame
traccia *f.n.* (*pl.* tracce)	trace, track
piacere *m.n.*	pleasure
treno *m.n.*	train
scientifico *adj.*	scientific
precedere	to precede (conjugated like temere)
immediato *adj.*	immediate
potente *adj.*	powerful, vigorous
eccellenza *f.n.*	excellence, excellency
metodo *m.n.*	method
intenzione *f.n.*	intention

visitare	to visit
personaggio *m.n.*	character
materiale *m.n.*	material
locale *adj.*	local
avvenimento *m.n.*	occurrence, event
risultare	to result
dente *m.n.*	tooth
tema *m.n.* (	subject
milione *num.*	million
dominare	to dominate
considerazione *f.n.*	consideration
biblioteca *f.n.*	library
scrittore *m.n.* (*f.n.* scrittrice)	writer
segretario *m.n.*	(m.) secretary
opportuno *adj.*	suitable
comunicare	to communicate
affidare	to entrust
influenza *f.n.*	influence

lezione *f.n.*	lesson
contadino *m.n.*	countryman
costituzione *f.n.*	constitution
ciascuno *pron.*	everyone
lieve *adj.*	light, soft
direzione *f.n.*	direction
eppure *conj.*	and yet
diffondere	to spread, diffuse
io diffondo	noi diffondiamo
tu diffendi	voi diffondete
lui diffende	loro diffondono
raro *adj.*	rare
amicizia *f.n.*	friendship
ala *f.n.*	wing
dono *m.n.*	gift
famoso *adj.*	famous
commissione *f.n.*	commission
esatto *adj.*	exact
accorrere	to rush (conjugated like correre)
costruzione *f.n.*	construction
disegno *m.n.*	drawing, design
soluzione *f.n.*	solution
sud *m.n.*	south

guidice *m.n.*	judge
commendatore *m.n.*	commander
costringere	to force
io constringo	noi constringiamo
tu costringi	voi costringete
lui costrige	loro costringono
finchè *conj.*	until, while
profondo *adj.*	deepest, lowest
genio *m.n.* (*pl.* geni)	genius, inclination
centrale *adj.*	central
misurare	to measure
Don *m.n.*	honorific for noblemen, priests and criminals
conclusione *f.n.*	conclusion
civile *adj.*	civil
tono *m.n.*	tone
meritare	to merit
giudizio *m.n.*	judgement
reale *adj.*	real, royal
terribile *adj.*	terrible
avvocato *m.n.*	lawyer (barrister, counsel and solicitor)
conquista *f.n.*	conquest
cavaliere *m.n.*	rider, knight
seguito *m.n.*	following, sequel

battaglia *f.n.*	battle
gesto *m.n.*	gesture
fianco *m.n.*	side
visita *f.n.*	visit
avanti *adv.*	before, forward
ricerca *f.n.*	research, enquiry
chilometro *m.n.*	kilometer
volgere	to turn (conjugated like svolgere)
ente *m.n.*	being, board
distinguere	to distinguish
io distinguo	noi distinguiamo
tu distingui	voi distinguete
lui distingue	loro distinguono
stampa *f.n.*	stamp, press, engraving
guardia *f.n.*	guard, protection
bambino *m.n.*	boy, child, lad
Rilevare	to take away, up, over
montagna *f.n.*	mountain
compagnia *f.n.*	company
estate *f.n.*	summer
commercio *m.n.*	commerce
prezioso *adj.*	precious
aumentare	to increase

progresso *m.n.*	progress
completo *adj.*	complete
pezzo *m.n.*	piece
vittoria *f.n.*	victory
piano *m.n.*	plan, level, scheme
suonare	to play, sound
caratteristico *adj.*	characteristic
risposta *f.n.*	reply
studioso *m.n.*	scholar
filosofia *f.n.*	philosophy
illuminare	to brighten, lighten
precisamente *adv.*	precisely
onda *f.n.*	wave
sfuggire	to escape, miss (conjugated like sentire)
discendere	to descend (conjugated like prendere
estero *m.n.*	foreign lands (andare all'estero, to go abrode)
contatto *m.n.*	contact
acquistare	to acquire
coscienza *f.n.*	conscience
filosofo *m.n.*	philosopher

croce *f.n.*	cross
classico *adj.*	classic(al)
impossibile *adj.*	impossible
glorioso *adj.*	glorious
comandare	to order, command
denaro *m.n.*	money
nave *f.n.*	ship, boat
esame *m.n.*	examination
artistico *adj.*	artistic
nebbia *f.n.*	fog, mist
argento *m.n.*	silver
atmosfera *f.n.*	atmosphere
domani *adv.*	tomorrow
esercito *m.n.*	army
gridare	to shout, shriek
probabilmente *adv.*	probably
agitare	to shake, excite
greco *adj.*	Greek
sezione *f.n.*	section
scorso *adj.*	past (la settimana scorsa, last week)

luminoso *adj.*	shining, luminous
inoltre *adv.*	moreover, besides
vendere	to sell (conjugated like temere)
sostanza *f.n.*	substance, riches
invitare	to invite
contento *adj.*	happy
badare	to take care, pay attention
essere *m.n.*	being, state
meraviglioso *adj.*	marvellous
operare	to operate, act
trascinare	to drag, draw
figlio *m.n.*	son, boy
latte *m.n.*	milk
solito *adj.*	usual
definitivo *adj.*	definitive
abbracciare	to embrace
stringere	to constrain, press (conjugated like constringere)
vuoto *adj.*	empty
qualsiasi *adv.*	whatever, whichever
godere	to enjoy
io godo	noi godiamo
tu godi	voi godete
lui gode	loro godono

specchio *m.n.*	mirror
internazionale *adj.*	international
compito *m.n.*	duty, homework
fenomeno *m.n.*	phenomenon
coppia *f.n.*	couple
modesto *adj.*	modest, humble
banco *m.n.*	bench, bank
falso *adj.*	false
discutere	to discuss
io discuto	noi discutiamo
tu discuti	voi discutete
lui discute	loro discutono
male *adj.*	bad, wrong
mistero *m.n.*	mystery
altezza *f.n.*	height (Sua Altezza, Your Highness)
tomba *f.n.*	tomb
finora *adv.*	as yet, hitherto
felicità *f.n.* (*pl.* felicità)	happiness
calmo *adj.*	calm
passaggio *m.n.*	passage
generale *m.n.*	general
cammino *m.n.*	way, path, journey
individuo *m.n.*	individual
metro *m.n.*	meter

contemporaneo *adj.*	contemporary
diretto *adj.*	direct
scomparire	to disappear (conjugated like apparire)
teoria *f.n.*	theory
abitare	to inhabit
buttare	to throw
vino *m.n.*	wine
intelligente *adj.*	intelligent
attuale *adj.*	current, real
tedesco *adj.*	German
perfettamente *adv.*	perfectly
rimettere	to replace, defer, remit (conjugated like mettere)
duro *adj.*	hard
determinare	to determine
sicurrezza *f.n.*	safety
trattato *m.n.*	treaty
ospite *m.n.*	host, guest
programma *m.n.* (*pl.* programmi)	programme
moto *m.n.*	movement, motion
spegnere	to put out, extinguish

<table>
<tr><td>io spengo</td><td>noi spegniamo</td></tr>
<tr><td>tu spegni</td><td>voi spegnete</td></tr>
<tr><td>lui spegne</td><td>loro spengono</td></tr>
</table>

sei *num.*	six
elettrico *adj.*	electric
istante *m.n.*	instant
negare	to deny
nord *m.n.*	north
medico *m.n.*	doctor
potere *m.n.*	power
lieto *adj.*	happy
processo *m.n.*	process, trial
sino *prep.*	until, as far as
parecchio *adj.*	very much, a lot
veste *f.n.*	garment, dress
educazione *f.n.*	education
derivare	to derive
capace *adj.*	capable, capacious
strappare	to tear away, root out
opporre	to oppose (conjugated like porre)
nuovo *adj.*	new
popolazione *f.n.*	population
cultura *f.n.*	culture

distanza *f.n.*	distance
cadavere *m.n.*	corpse
otto *num.*	eight
addirittura *adj.*	absolutely
sposare	to marry
capitare	to happen
orizzonte *m.n.*	horizon
rispetto *m.n.*	respect
poichè *conj.*	since, now that
regione *f.n.*	region
straniero *adj.*	foreigner
illusione *f.n.*	illusion
pronunciare	to pronounce
grandezza *f.n.*	greatness, size
sano *adj.*	healthy, sane
francese *m.n., f.n.*	Frenchman, Frenchwoman
lanciare	to throw, launch
ingegnere *m.n.*	engineer
attaccare	to attack, attach
sette *num.*	seven

doloroso *adj.*	painful, sore
valle *f.n.*	valley
pianura *f.n.*	plain
stanco *adj.*	tired
capello *m.n.*	hair (s.) (farsi tagliare i capelli, to have one's hair cut)
ritmo *m.n.*	rhythm
particolarmente *adv.*	particularly
provocare	to provoke
abbastanza *adj.*	sufficient
tradizione *f.n.*	tradition
lontano *adv.*	afar, distantly
legno *m.n.*	wood, log
acuto *adj.*	acute
ve *pron.*	you, to you
repubblica *f.n.*	republic
ambiente *m.n.*	surroundings
conceszione *f.n.*	conception
scoppiare	to break out, explode
merito *m.n.*	merit, worth
bacio *m.n.*	kiss
raggio *m.n.*	ray

rompere	to break
io rompo	noi rompiamo
tu rompi	voi rompete
lui rompe	loro rompono
medio *adj.*	middle, average
spirituale *adj.*	spiritual
fondare	to found
ammirare	to admire
intenso *adj.*	intense
divino *adj.*	divine
serie *f.n.*	series
bile *f.n.*	bile, bad temper
massa *f.n.*	mass
nudo *adj.*	naked
rivedere	to see again, revise (arriverderci!, goodbye!) (conjugated like vedere)
poichè *conj.*	since, because
caffè *m.n.*	coffee
tirare	to pull, draw, shoot at
margine *m.n.*	margin, edge
pane *m.n.*	bread, loaf
assolutamente *adv.*	absolutely
imperatore *m.n.*	emperor
cane *m.n.* (*f.* cagna, bitch)	dog
senatore *m.n.*	senator

fondamentale *adj.*	fundamental
amante *m.n., f.n.*	lover
militare *adj.*	military
pranzo *m.n.*	dinner (colloquially, luncheon)
facilmente *adv.*	easily
industriale *adj.*	industrial
arrivo *m.n.*	arrival
riempire	to fill (in) (conjugated like capire and temere)
turbare	to trouble
ragazza *f.n.*	girl
eseguire	to execute, perform (conjugated like capire)
sale *m.n.*	salt
petto *m.n.*	chest, breast
pioggia *f.n.*	rain
confessare	to confess
prodotto *m.n.*	product, produce
indagine *f.n.*	enquiry, research
sostituire	to substitute (conjugated like capire)
ipotesi *f.n.*	hypothesis

cima *f.n.* — top, peak

descrivere — to describe (conjugated like scrivere)

unità *f.n.* (*pl.* unità) — unity, unit

certezza *f.n.* — certainty

quantità *f.n.* (*pl.* quantità) — quantity

eterno *adj.* — eternal

poesia *f.n.* — poem, poetry

costume *m.n.* — costume, custom

grazioso *adj.* — gentle, charming, gracious

documento *m.n.* — document

iniziativa *f.n.* — initiative

circostanza *f.n.* — circumstance

vestire — to dress, put on (mi vesto subito, I'll get dressed now) (conjugated like sentire)

letteratura *f.n.* — literature

istinto *m.n.* — instinct

invito *m.n.* — invitation

dramma *m.n.* (*pl.* drammi) — drama

minimo *adj.* — least

oltre *prep.*	beyond, besides
bambina *f.n.*	little girl
ringraziare	to thank
mercato *m.n.*	market
avanzare	to advance, put forward
corrente *f.n.*	current, stream
gentile *adj.*	polite, kind
consentire	to agree (conjugated like sentire)
inizio *m.n.*	beginning
ladro *m.n.*	thief
vecchio *m.n.*	old (man)
provincia *f.n.*	province (in provincia, in the country)
duca *m.n.* (*pl.* duchi) (*f.* duchessa)	duke
pratica *f.n.*	experience
umile *adj.*	humble
monumento *m.n.*	monument
precedente *adj.*	preceding
nerverso *adj.*	nervous
mattino *m.n.*	morning

morto *adj.*	dead
regno *m.n.*	kingdom, reign
lago *m.n.*	lake
agire	to act (conjugated like capire)
prossimo *adj.*	next
lento *adj.*	slow
carità *f.n.* (*pl.* carità)	charity
giovinezza *f.n.*	youth
colpire	to strike (conjugated like capire)
operazione *f.n.*	operation
nominare	to nominate, name
percorrere	to travel, cover (conjugated like correre)
cervello *m.n.*	brain
attesa *f.n.*	expectation (sala d'attesa, waiting room)
ferire	to wound (conjugated like capire)
rientrare	to return home, re-enter
rete *f.n.*	net (work)
arrestare	to arrest, stop
male *adv.*	badly

penetrare	to penetrate
resistenza *f.n.*	resistance
differenza *f.n.*	difference
relativo *adj.*	relative
contrasto *m.n.*	contrast
elevare	to raise
affetto *m.n.*	affection
rivoluzione *f.n.*	revolution
cessare	to cease
tesoro *m.n.*	treasure, treasury
opinione *f.n.*	opinion
proseguire	to continue, pursue (conjugated like seguire)
strumento *m.n.*	instrument
dedicare	to dedicate
perdita *f.n.*	loss
rilievo *m.n.*	relief
vittima *f.n.*	victim
parente *m.n.*	relative
sospetto *m.n.*	suspect person, suspicion
conte *m.n.* (*f.* contessa)	count

autorità *f.n.* (*pl.* autorità)	authority
suolo *m.n.*	soil, ground
pomeriggio *m.n.*	afternoon
guidare	to guide
evidente *adj.*	evident
cappello *m.n.*	hat
sorriso *m.n*	smile
mezzogiorno *m.n.*	midday, south
neanche *adv.*	not even
comunicazione *f.n.*	communication
prestare	to lend, render
titolo *m.n.*	title
febbre *f.n.*	fever
preghiera *f.n.*	prayer
giugno *m.n.*	June
data *f.n.*	date
eroe *m.n.*	hero
subire	to suffer, undergo (conjugated like sentire)
violento *adj.*	violent

conversazione *f.n.*	conversation
mille *num.*	thousand
europeo *adj.*	European
imparare	to learn
a lungo *adv.*	slowly, tediously
detto *adj.*	said
fisso *adj.*	fixed
precipatare	to hasten, hurl down
spazio *m.n.*	space
biglietto *m.n.*	ticket
secco *adj.*	dry
direttamente *adv.*	directly
innanzi *prep.*	before
essere abituati	to be accustomed
bosco *m.n.*	wood
significare	to mean
lungo *prep.*	along
comperare	to buy
bruno *adj.*	brown
fiducia *f.n.*	confidence, trust

mestiere *m.n.*	job, occupation
esercitare	to exercise
ragionare	to discuss
armonia *f.n.*	harmony
fiamma *f.n.*	flame
convincere	to convince (conjugated like vincere)
castello *m.n.*	castle
insomma *adv.*	briefly, in short
spesa *f.n.*	expense, shopping
dapprima *adv.*	at first
volare	to fly
oriente *m.n.*	east, Orient
alba *f.n.*	dawn
cittadino *m.n.*	citizen
suo *pron.*	his own, her own (dalla sua, on his side)
pericoloso *adj.*	dangerous
curiosità *f.n.* (*pl.* curiosità)	curiosity
cupo *adj.*	dark, deep, hollow
trattenere	to hold back, detain (conjugated like tenere)
manifestazione *f.n.*	manifestation, exhibition

raccomandare	to recommend, entrust (posta raccomandata, registered post)
povero *m.n.*	pauper, poor man
grano *m.n.*	grain, corn
gloria *f.n.*	glory
confronto *m.n.*	comparison
regola *f.n.*	rule, regulation
lassù *adv.*	up there
stasera *adv.*	tonight
fatto *adj.*	made, grown
crisi *f.n.*	crisis
allegro *adj.*	lively, merry
bruciare	to burn
rosa *f.n.*	rose
indipendenza *f.n.*	independence
ospedale *m.n.*	hospital
edificio *m.n.*	building
ruota *f.n.*	wheel
scambio *m.n.*	exchange
cogliere	to pick, take (conjugated like raccogliere)

svegliare	to rouse, wake up
esaminare	to examine
tuttora *adv.*	still, again
responsabile *adv.*	responsible
favore *m.n.*	favour
solenne *adj.*	solemn
colonna *f.n.*	column
impresa *f.n.*	enterprise, firm
invocare	to invoke
splendore *m.n.*	brightness
odore *m.n.*	smell
collocare	to place, dispose of
buio *m.n.*	darkness
accostare	to accost
ufficiale *m.n.*	official, officer
altrettanto *adv.*	as many, as much (altrettanto! the same to you!)
pallido *adj.*	pale
cenno *m.n.*	sign, mention
applicazione *f.n.*	application
sciogliere	to dissolve, loosen (conjugated like raccogliere)

porto *m.n.* — port
ingresso *m.n.* — entrance
organizzazione *f.n.* — organisation
destra *f.n.* — right (hand)
tragic *adj.* — tragic
supporre — to suppose (conjugated like porre)

categoria *f.n.* — category
pianta *f.n.* — plant, map
complicato *adj.* — complicated
scarso *adj.* — scarce, insufficient
calma *f.n.* — Calm, quiet
attacco *m.n.* — attack
marmo *m.n.* — marble
provenire — to derive, proceed (conjugated like venire)

evidentemente *adv.* — evidently
procurare — to obtain, attempt
fornire — to furnish, provide with (conjugated like capire)

orientale *adj.* — eastern, oriental
respiro *m.n.* — breath
tremare — to tremble

immobile *adj.*	motionless (beni immobili, real estate)
consistere	to consist of (conjugated like esistere)
scambiare	to exchange
cimitero *m.n.*	cemetery
adoperare	to use
progetto *m.n.*	project
pubblicazione *f.n.*	publication
unire	to join, connect (conjugated like raggiungere)
rapidamente *adv.*	rapidly
chiarire	to clarify, explain (conjugated like capire)
prevedere	to foresee, expect (conjugated like vedere)
giocare	to play
consigliare	to advise
umido *adj.*	wet, humid
attimo *m.n.*	moment
proprietario *m.n.*	owner
avvenire	to happen, occur (conjugated like venire)
orologio *m.n.*	clock
cortile *m.n.*	courtyard
domenica *f.n.*	Sunday

abitudine *f.n.*	habit
domino *m.n.*	domino (mask), dominoes
giovare	to benefit, be of use
collegio *m.n.*	college
miracolo *m.n.*	miracle
indipendente *adj.*	independent
contribuire	to contribute (conjugated like capire)
dio *m.n.* (*pl.* gli dei)	god, God
confine *m.n.*	frontier, limit
naso *m.n.*	nose
coraggio *m.n.*	courage
escludere	to exclude (conjugated like chiudere)
partito *m.n.*	party, side
gatto *m.n.*	cat
riposo *m.n.*	rest
consegnare	to deliver
colonnello *m.n.*	colonel
prato *m.n.*	meadow
viaggiatore *m.n.*	traveller

sviluppare	to develop
vestito *m.n.*	dress, suit
citare	to cite
modello *m.n.*	model
dicembre *m.n.*	December
da cui *adv.*	whence, by which
unito *adj.*	united
lettore *m.n.* (*f.* lettrice)	reader
membro *m.n.* (*f.pl.* in anatomy, le membra)	member
labbro *m.n.* (*f.pl.* le labbra)	lip
costo *m.n.*	cost
vuoto *adj.*	empty, void
tè *m.n.*	tea
costa *f.n.*	coast
agosto *m.n.*	August
fedele *adj.*	faithful
interno *adj.*	inner, interior
fase *f.n.*	phase

piegare	to fold
sensibilità *f.n.* (*pl.* sensibilità)	sensibility
lusso *m.n.*	luxury, extravagance
presidente *m.n.*	president
velo *m.n.*	veil
intelligenza f.n.	intelligence
stamattina *adv.*	this morning
partenza *f.n.*	departure
impero *m.n.*	empire
coloniale *adj.*	colonial
destinare	to destine, address (a letter)
vicenda *f.n.*	event, turn
trenta *num.*	thirty
volo *m.n.*	flight
arco *m.n.*	arch, bow
lentamente *adv.*	slowly
cattolico *adv.*	Catholic
zio *m.n.*	uncle
insegnamento *m.n.*	teaching

richiedere	to send for, require (conjugated like chiedere)
corsa *f.n.*	race, run
ritratto *m.n.*	portrait
continuare	to continue, follow up
trincea *f.n.*	trench
sorprendere	to surprise (conjugated like prendere)
straniero *m.n.*	foreigner
trasformare	to transform
fortuna *f.n.*	luck, fortune
organo *m.n.*	organ
tristezza *f.n.*	sadness
tenero *adj.*	tender
cacciare	to hunt, banish, drive away
promettere	to promise (conjugated like mettere)
cameriera *f.n.*	waitress, chambermaid
orgoglio *m.n.*	pride
sempre *adj.*	ever
commettere	to commit (conjugated like mettere)
vago *adj.*	indistinct, erratic, charming
paterno *adj.*	paternal
velocità *f.n.* (*pl.* velocità)	speed

esterno *adj.*	outer, exterior
promessa *f.n.*	promise
indirizzo *m.n.*	address
freddo *adj.*	cold
separare	to separate
celebre *adj.*	celebrated
atteggiamento *m.n.*	attitude, behaviour
rigido *adj.*	rigid
articolo *m.n.*	article
primitivo *adj.*	primitive
elegante *adj.*	elegant
catena *f.n.*	chain
cinema *m.n.*	cinema
tentativo *m.n.*	attempt
lavoratore *m.n.* (*f.* lavoratrice)	worker
rumore *m.n.*	noise
maschera *f.n.*	mask
ingannare	to deceive
specie *adv.*	especially
radio *f.n.*	radio, broadcasting

banca *f.n.*	bank
economia *f.n.*	economy, economics
rinnovare	to renew
carica *f.n.*	charge, employment
ingegno *m.n.*	genius, talent
centinaio *m.n.* (*f.pl.* centinaia)	hundred
pastore *m.n.*	shepherd
determinato *adj.*	stated, definite
romanzo *m.n.*	novel
collega *m.n., f.n.* (*pl.* colleghi)	colleague
fascio *m.n.*	bunch, bundle, sheaf
meraviglia *f.n.*	marvel
accusare	to accuse
corda *f.n.*	rope, string
miseria *f.n.*	misery, penury
immediatamente *adv.*	immediately
resistere	to resist (conjugated like esistere)
originale *adj.*	original
latino *adj.*	Latin

blocco *m.n.*	block
richiamo *m.n.*	recall, summons
seno *m.n.*	bosom
partecipare	to participate
servo *m.n.*	servant
dignità *f.n.* (*pl.* dignità)	dignity, self-respect
staccare	to detach, pull off
rivista *f.n.*	review, magazine
misterioso *adj.*	mysterious
novembre *m.n.*	November
privato *adj.*	private
riva *f.n.*	bank, shore
stesso *pron.*	oneself, himself, herself
simbolo *m.n.*	symbol
fila *f.n.*	row
superficie *f.n.* (*pl.* superfici, superficie)	surface
punta *f.n.*	point, tip
messa *f.n.*	mass
constatare	to ascertain, establish

contributo *m.n.*	contribution
affrontare	to confront, face
barba *f.n.*	beard
prezzo *m.n.*	price
qualunque *adj.*	whatever
carro *m.n.*	cart, van
definire	to define, resolve (conjugated like finire)
condannare	to condemn
fattore *m.n.*	agent
continente *m.n.*	continent
sacrificio *m.n.*	sacrifice
incominciare	to begin
ottobre *m.n.*	October
grigio *adj.*	grey
vestito *adj.*	dressed
lucido *adj.*	bright, brilliant
odio *m.n.*	hate, hatred
critico *adj.*	critical
aprile *m.n.*	April
assegnare	to assign, grant

moda *f.n.*	fashion
respingere	to repel, repulse
io respingo	noi respingiamo
tu respingi	voi respingete
lui respinge	loro respingono
comitato *m.n.*	committee
fango *m.n.*	mud
commerciale *adj.*	commercial
fabbrica *f.n.*	factory
singolo *adj.*	single
Ispirare	to inspire
santo *m.n.*	saint
Introdurre	to introduce (conjugated like ridurre)
disciplina *f.n.*	discipline
Informare	to inform
nido *m.n.*	nest
oppure *adv.*	or
stupore *m.n.*	amazement
onorevole *m.n.*	parliament deputy
dato *m.n.*	fact
disgrazia *f.n.*	disgrace, accident
ammirazione *f.n.*	admiration
suggerire	to suggest (conjugated like capire)

frequente *adj.*	frequent
richiesta *f.n.*	request, demand
contenuto *m.n.*	contents
commozione *f.n.*	emotion, commotion
trascurare	to disregard, overlook
raccolta *f.n.*	collection, harvest
girare	to turn, change round
grandioso *adj.*	majestic, stately
abbassare	to lower, reduce
soglia *f.n.*	threshold
chiave *f.n.*	key
regolare	to regulate
sensazione *f.n.*	sensation
seta *f.n.*	silk
aumento *m.n.*	increase
severo *adj.*	severe
vergogna *f.n.*	shame
congresso *m.n.*	congress
sedia *f.n.*	chair, seat
abbandono *m.n.*	abandonment, waiving
comparire	to appear, attend (conjugated like apparire)

curioso *adj.*	curious
dottrina *f.n.*	doctrine
fama *f.n.*	fame, reputation
americano *adj.*	American
esaltare	to exalt, extol
formazione *f.n.*	formation, creation
salute *f.n.*	health, welfare
inferiore *adj.*	lower, inferior
maschio *m.n.*	male
informazione *f.n.*	information
scorgere	to perceive (conjugated like sorgere)
affacciare	to indicate
voglia *f.n.*	wish, desire
statua *f.n.*	statue
sebbene *adv.*	even less
dimostrazione *f.n.*	demonstration
comodo *adj.*	comfortable
ministero *m.n.*	ministry
deporre	to deposit, depose (conjugated like porre)
retta *f.n.*	straight line

estendere	to extend (conjugated like prendere)
polvere *f.n.*	dust, powder
scorrere	to glide, glance at, elapse (conjugated like correre)
netto *adj.*	clean, clear (prezzo netto, net price)
fonte *f.n.*	source, fountain
basilica *f.n.*	basilica
futuro *adj.*	future
peggio *adv.*	worse
spiegazione *f.n.*	explanation
tronco *m.n.*	trunk
conferenza *f.n.*	lecture, conference
cerchio *m.n.*	circle
stile *m.n.*	style
ricordare	to recall, remind
entrambi *pron.*	both
indispensabile *adj.*	indispensable
volentieri *adv.*	willingly
odiare	to hate
osservatore *m.n.* (*f.* osservatrice)	observer

scarpa *f.n.*	shoe
capitolo *m.n.*	chapter
settembre *m.n.*	September
bravo *adj.*	good, able, plucky, clever
altrimenti *adv.*	otherwise
personale *adj.*	personal
avvolgere	to roll up (conjugated like svolgere)
scritto *m.n.*	writing
risalire	to rise (again) trace back (conjugated like salire)
simpatico *adj.*	nice, pleasant
divertire	to amuse, entertain (conjugated like sentire)
spargere	to spread, scatter
io spargo	noi spargiamo
tu spargi	voi spargete
lui sparge	loro spargono
novità (*pl.* novità)	novelty
capitale *m.n. f.* capital,	capital (financial), capital (city)
miglio *m.n.*	mile, millet
danno *m.n.*	damage, injury
distribuire	to distribute (conjugated like partire)
complesso *adj.*	complex

metallico *adj.*	metallic
fiero *adj.*	proud, fierce
prigione *f.n.*	prison
facoltà *f.n.* (*pl.* facoltà)	faculty
gamba *f.n.*	leg
distinto *adj.*	distinguished, refined
soffocare	to suffocate
fisico *adj.*	physical
amministrazione *f.n.*	administration
rovesciare	to overthrow, overturn
talvolta *adv.*	sometimes
provvedimento *m.n.*	precaution
tecnica *f.n.*	technique
unione *f.n.*	union
racconto *m.n.*	story
camicia *f.n.*	shirt
formula *f.n.*	formula
visione *f.n.*	vision
guaio *m.n.*	woe, fix

fotografia *f.n.*	photograph(y)
tempo *m.n.*	time
malato *adj.*	ill
complesso *m.n.*	complex
paradiso *m.n.*	paradise
meravigliare	to marvel
paura *m.n.*	fear, dread
vizio *m.n.*	vice
quarto *m.n.*	quarter
sonno *m.n.*	sleep
dito *m.n.* (*pl.* usu. *f.* le dita)	finger
convincere	to persuade
io convinco	noi convinciamo
tu convinci	voi convincete
lui convince	loro convincono
bestia *f.n.*	beast
consumare	to wear out, consume
là *adv.*	there
preparazione *f.n.*	preparation
invece *prep.*	instead
finite *adj.*	finished
femmina *f.n.*	female, woman

fuga *f.n.*	flight, escape
laggiù *adv.*	down there
norma *f.n.*	rule, norm, guidance
missione *f.n.*	mission
coro *m.n.*	chorus
legato *adj.*	bound, tied
collina *f.n.*	hill
azzurro *adj.*	blue
sparire	to disappear (conjugated like apparire)
scandalo *m.n.*	scandal
trascorrere	to spend (time) (conjugated like correre)
febbraio *m.n.*	February
sasso *m.n.*	stone
gioventù *f.n.* (*pl.* gioventù)	young people, youth
frutta *f.n.* (*pl.* frutta, frutte)	fruit
rifare	to do again, rebuild
fumo *m.n.*	smoke

magari *adv.*	maybe, if only
ballo *m.n.*	ball, dance
eccezionale *adj.*	exceptional
ansia *f.n.*	anxiety
piovere	to rain (only 3rd person sg. of each tense; conjugated like bere)
maturo *adj.*	ripe
cedere	to yield
io cedo	noi cediamo
tu cedi	voi cedete
lui cede	loro cedono
essenzialmente *adv.*	essentially
diminuire	to diminish, reduce (conjugated like capire)
Papa *m.n.* (*pl.* i papi)	pope
improvvisamente *adv.*	suddenly
dipendere	to depend (conjugated like prendere)
ironia *f.n.*	irony
accanto *adv.*	close by, nearby
lampada *f.n.*	lamp
semplicemente *adv.*	simply
universitario *adj.*	academic
solido *adj.*	solid
cinquanta *num.*	fifty

calore *m.n.*	heat
distribuire	to distribute (conjugated like capire)
sincero *adj.*	sincere
accelerare	to quicken
uguale *adj.*	equal
domestico *adj.*	domestic
silenzioso *adj.*	silent
materiale *adj.*	material
siccome *conj.*	since, as
telegramma *m.n.* (*pl.* telegrammi)	telegram
vetro *m.n.*	glass
patto *m.n.*	pact
finire	to finish, terminate
adottare	to adopt
protagonista *m.n.* (*pl.* protagonisti)	protagonist
impiegare	to employ
privo *adj.*	lacking, devoid

normale *adj.*	normal
logica *f.n.*	logic
essenziale *adj.*	essential
marchese *m.n.* (*f.* marchesa)	marquis
verso *m.n.*	(line of) verse
migliaio *m.n.* (*pl.* migliaia)	thousand
sinistra *adj.*	left
omaggio *m.n.*	homage
colei *pron.*	she who
forno *m.n.*	oven, furnace
caccia *f.n.*	hunt(ing)
villaggio *m.n.*	village
perdonare	to forgive
genitore *m.n.* (*f.* genitrice)	parent
conquistare	to conquer
mortale *adj.*	mortal
criterio *m.n.*	criterion, standard
scuro *adj.*	dark

indicazione *f.n.*	indication
combattere	to fight (conjugated like temere)
innocente *adj.*	innocent
umore *m.n.*	humour
nuvola *f.n.*	cloud
fame *f.n.*	hunger
acceso *adj.*	lit
cerimonia *f.n.*	ceremony
recentemente *adv.*	recently
doppio *adj.*	double
cassa *f.n.*	box, case, cashier's desk
terzo *m.n.*	third
rubare	to steal
compagna *f.n.*	(female) partner
sostare	to pause, stop
continuamente *adv.*	continually, continuously
ultimo *pron.*	last
corte *f.n.*	court(yard)
eleganza *f.n.*	elegance

violenza *f.n.*	violence
costante *adj.*	constant
religione *f.n.*	religion
fretta *f.n.*	haste
tesi *f.n.* (*pl.* tesi)	thesis
saltare	to jump
diavolo *m.n.*	devil
abbastanza *adv.*	enough, sufficiently
lembo *m.n.*	edge, border
dimensione *f.n.*	dimension
sentimentale *adj.*	sentimental
arabo *adj.*	Arab, Arabic
furia *f.n.*	fury
circondare	to surround
leggenda *f.n.*	legend
vaso *m.n.*	pot, vase
campana *f.n.*	bell
cancello *m.n.*	railing, gate
aspro *adj.*	harsh, tart

tracciare	to trace
subito *adj.*	sudden
occidentale *adj.*	western
segreto *m.n.*	secret
inviare	to send
coperto *adj.*	covered
ulteriore *adj.*	further, ulterior
commuovere, commovere	to affect, excite (conjugated like muovere)
regolare *adj.*	regular
realmente *adv.*	really, royally
marittimo *adj.*	maritime
neve *f.n.*	snow
esercizio *m.n.*	excercise
sfruttare	to exploit, exhaust
dettare	to dictate
ricominciare	to start again
uccello *m.n.*	bird
provvisorio *adj.*	provisional, temporary
oh! *interj.*	oh!
suscitare	to provoke, rouse

qualche *adj.* — some
inoltre *adv.* — also, likewise
fascista *adj.* — fascist
solco *m.n.* — furrow, wake (of ship)
tecnico *adj.* — technical
tetto *m.n.* — roof
reggere — to rule, support, endure (conjugated like leggere)

capitano *m.n.* — captain
tradurre — to translate (conjugated like ridurre)

debito *m.n.* — debt
difetto *m.n.* — defect
opposto *adj.* — opposite, contrary
esperimento *m.n.* — experiment, trial
devoto *adj.* — pious, devout
perduto *adj.* — lost
individuale *adj.* — individual
incoraggiare — to encourage
generazione *f.n.* — generation
intorno *adv.* — around
debole *adj.* — weak

regina *f.n.*	queen
maestà *f.n.* (*pl.* maestà)	majesty
lavare	to wash
diffuso *adj.*	diffuse, broadcast
critica *f.n.*	criticism
positivo *adj.*	positive
prigioniero *m.n.*	prisoner
premere	to press, urge (conjugated like temere)
sepolcro *m.n.*	tomb, vault
vicinanza *f.n.*	neighbourhood
solito *m.n.*	usual (fuori dal solito, out of the ordinary)
reciproco *adj.*	reciprocal
amoroso *adj.*	amorous
personalità *f.n.* (*pl.* Personalità)	personality
eco *f. n.* (*pl.* gli echi)	echo
canale *m.n.*	canal, channel (but la Manica, English Channel
ginocchio *m.n.* (*pl.* le ginocchia)	knee

ardente *adj.*	burning
sacco *m.n.*	sack, bag
celeste *adj.*	heavenly, sky-blue
sparare	to shoot, fire
risvegliare	to awake, stir
senato *m.n.*	senate
apparecchio *m.n.*	apparatus
sinistro *adj.*	left, ominous
gennaio *m.n.*	January
carico *m.n.*	load, charge
incontro *prep.*	towards
sposa *f.n.*	bride
promuovere	to promote (conjugated like commuovere)
giovanile *adj.*	juvenile
simpatia *f.n.*	sympathy, liking
roccia *f.n.* (*pl.* rocce)	rock
apparenza *f.n.*	appearance
avventura *f.n.*	adventure
issustrare	to illustrate
bianco *m.n.*	white, white man

sorpresa *f.n.*	surprise
paesaggio *m.n.*	landscape
mancanza *f.n.*	lack, absence
incerto *adj.*	uncertain
prima *f.n.*	first (class), première
eccezione *f.n.*	exception
matrimonio *m.n.*	marriage, wedding
reparto *m.n.*	department, (military) detachment
robusto *adj.*	robust, strong
sconosciuto *adj.*	unknown
assorbire	to absorb (conjugated like capire)
gola *f.n.*	throat
tenerezza *f.n.*	tenderness
logico *adj.*	logical
tensione *f.n.*	tension
onorevole *adj.*	honourable
vano *adj.*	vain
collaborazione *f.n.*	collaboration
calmare	to calm
disegnare	to draw, design

ITALIAN
INDEX

a	1	affrontare	82	anche	2
a lungo	69	aggiungere	26	ancora	4
a proposito	32	agire	66	andare	4
abbandonare	33	agitare	55	angolo	38
abbandono	84	agosto	76	anima	12
abbassare	84	ah!	42	animale	36
abbastanza	61,95	aiutare	46	animo	48
abbracciare	56	aiuto	46	anno	3
abitare	58	ala	51	ansia	91
abito	42	alba	70	antico	14
abitudine	75	albergo	43	anzi	10
accanto	32, 91	albero	33	aperto	23
accelerare	92	alcuno	7, 47	apparecchio	99
accendere	48	allegro	71	apparenza	99
accennare	42	allontanare	47	apparire	11
acceso	94	allora	6	appartenere	39
accettare	27	almeno	16	appena	15
accogliere	37	altezza	57	applicazione	72
accompagnare	16	alto	8, 39	appoggiare	49
accordo	26	altra	3	appunto	41
accorgersi	42	altrettanto	72	aprile	82
accorrere	51	altrimenti	87	aprire	11
accostare	72	altro	3, 5	arabo	95
accusare	80	alzare	33	arco	77
acqua	10	amante ,	63	ardente	99
acquistare	54	amare	18	argento	55
acuto	61	ambiente	61	argomento	26
addirittura	60	americano	85	aria	11
adesso	47	amicizia	51	arma	46
adoperare	74	amico	15	armonia	70
adottare	92	ammettere	36	arrestare	66
affacciare	85	amministrazione	88	arrivare	9
affare	34	ammirare	62	arrivare	13
affatto	46	ammirazione	83	arrivo	63
affermare	46	amore	10	arte	16
affetto	67	amoroso	98	articolo	79
affidare	50	ampio	39	artista	40

artistico	55	avvenire	17, 74	bravo	87
ascoltare	23	avventura	99	breve	21
aspettare	14	avvertire	23	bruciare	71
aspetto	22	avvicinare	37	bruno	69
aspro	95	avvocato	52	brutto	47
assai	27, 29	avvolgere	87	buio	72
assegnare	82	azione	15	buono	7
assicurare	29	azzurro	90	buttare	58
assistere	48	baciare	45	caccia	93
assolutamente	62	bacio	61	cacciare	78
assoluto	46	badare	56	cadavere	60
assorbire	100	ballo	91	cadere	15
assumere	34	bambina	65	caffè	62
atmosfera	55	bambino	25, 53	caldo	26
attaccare	60	banca	80	calma	73
attacco	73	banco	57	calmare	100
atteggiamento	79	barba	82	calmo	57
attendere	25	base	45	calore	92
attenzione	36	basilica	86	cambiare	40
attesa	66	basso	24	camera	13
attimo	74	bastare	17	cameriera	78
attività	31	battaglia	53	camicia	88
atto	22	battere	42	camminare	41
attorno	43	bellezza	45	cammino	57
attraversare	48	bello	6	campagna	29
attraverso	17	bene	7, 27	campana	95
attuale	58	bere	38	campo	14
aumentare	53	bestia	89	canale	98
aumento	84	bianco	24, 99	cancello	95
automobile	24	biblioteca	50	cane	62
autore	22	biglietto	69	cantare	36
autorità	68	bile	62	canto	41
avanti	53	bisogno	19	capace	59
avanzare	65	blocco	81	capello	61
aver bisogno di	11	bocca	24	capire	16
avere	1	bosco	69	capitale	87
avvenimento	50	braccio	18	capitano	97

debito	97	dignità	81	divino	62
debole	97	dimensione	95	documento	64
decidere	32	dimenticare	27	dolce	35
dedicare	67	diminuire	91	dolore	29
definire	82	dimostrare	18	doloroso	61
definitivo	56	dimostrazione	85	domanda	41
degno	48	dinanzi	32	domandare	21
delicato	38	dio	75	domani	55
denaro	55	dipendere	91	domenica	74
dente	50	dire	2	domestico	92
dentro	31, 34	direttamente	69	dominare	50
deporre	85	diretto	58	domino	75
derivare	59	direttore	38	donna	8
descrivere	64	direzione	51	dono	51
desiderare	38	dirigere	47	dopo	5
desiderio	27	diritto	17	doppio	94
destinare	77	discendere	54	dormire	35
destino	37	disciplina	83	dottore	22
destra	73	discorso	20	dottrina	85
determinare	58	discussion	40	dove	5, 35
determinato	80	discutere	57	dovere	2
dettare	96	disegnare	100	dovere	31
detto	69	disegno	51	dramma	64
devoto	97	disgrazia	83	dubbio	27
di	1	disporre	31	duca	65
diavolo	95	disposizione	38	due	3, 28
dicembre	76	distanza	60	dunque	13
dichiarare	48	distinguere	53	durante	13
dieci	25	distinto	88	durare	20
dietro	26	distribuire	87, 89	duro	58
difendere	42	distruggere	42	e	1
difetto	97	dito	89	eccellenza	49
differenza	67	divenire	30	eccetera	33
difficile	30	diventare	11	eccezionale	91
difficoltà	34	diverso	12	eccezione	100
diffondere	51	divertire	87	ecco	23
diffuso	98	dividere	34		

eco	98	espressione	25	fatto	9, 71
economia	80	esprimere	33	fattore	82
economico	37	essa	6	favore	72
edificio	71	essenziale	93	febbraio	90
educazione	59	essenzialmente	91	febbre	68
effetto	26	essere	1, 56	fede	24
egli	5	essere abituati	69	fedele	76
elegante	79	esso	6	felice	18
eleganza	94	estate	53	felicità	57
element	23	estendere	86	femmina	89
elettrico	59	esterno	79	fenomeno	57
elevare	67	estero	54	ferire	66
energia	49	estremo	42	fermare	19
enorme	42	età	22	fermo	26
ente	53	eterno	64	ferro	36
entrambi	86	europeo	69	festa	26
entrare	10	evidente	68	fiamma	70
entro	39	evidentemente	73	fianco	53
epoca	48	evitare	38	fiducia	69
eppure	51	fabbrica	83	fiero	88
eroe	68	faccia	19	figlio	10, 56
errore	41	facile	29	figura	15
esaltare	85	facilmente	63	fila	81
esame	55	facoltà	88	filo	47
esaminare	72	falso	57	filosofia	54
esatto	51	fama	85	filosofo	54
escludere	75	fame	94	finalmente	35
eseguire	63	famiglia	12	finchè	52
esempio	16	famoso	51	fine	25
esercitare	70	fango	83	finestra	32
esercito	55	fantasia	49	finire	14, 92
esercizio	96	fare	2	finite	89
esistenza	42	fascio	80	fino	12, 20
esistere	13	fascista	97	finora	57
esperienza	30	fase	76	fiore	27
esperimento	97	fatica	46	fisico	88
esporre	42			fissare	32

leggero	34	
legno	61	
lei	11, 25	
lembo	95	
lentamente	77	
lento	66	
lettera	16	
letteratura	64	
letto	34	
lettore	76	
levare	34	
lezione	51	
li	6	
lì	17	
liberare	37	
libero	20	
libertà	35	
libro	14	
lieto	59	
lieve	51	
limitare	38	
limite	39	
linea	20	
lingua	27	
lira	31	
lo	1, 2	
locale	50	
logica	93	
logico	100	
lontano	15, 61	
loro	3, 9	
lotta	39	
luce	10	
lucido	82	
lui	5	
luminoso	56	
luna	45	
lungo	14, 69	
luogo	11	
lusso	77	
ma	2	
macchina	33	
madre	12	
maestà	98	
maestro	36	
magari	91	
maggio	47	
maggiore	11	
mai	7	
malato	89	
malattia	43	
male	28, 57, 66	
mamma	36	
mancanza	100	
mancare	16	
mandare	22	
mangiare	32	
maniera	37	
manifestare	43	
manifestazione	70	
mano	8	
mantenere	27	
marchese	93	
mare	9	
margine	62	
marito	17	
marittimo	96	
marmo	73	
maschera	79	
maschio	85	
massa	62	
massimo	26	
materiale	50, 92	
matrimonio	100	
mattina	26	
mattino	65	
maturo	91	
me	9	
medesimo	42	
medico	59	
medio	62	
mediterraneo	44	
meglio	17	
membro	76	
memoria	27	
meno	18, 22	
mente	32	
mentre	9, 20	
meraviglia	80	
meravigliare	89	
meraviglioso	56	
mercato	65	
meritare	52	
merito	61	
mese	12	
messa	81	
mestiere	70	
metà	25	
metallico	88	
metodo	49	
metro	57	
mettere	6	
mezzo	21, 26	
mezzogiorno	68	
mi	5	
mia	3	
migliaio	93	
miglio	87	
migliore	27	

quadro	43	rapporto	24	richiamare	47
qualche	5, 97	rappresentare	12	richiamo	81
qualcosa	39	raro	51	richiedere	78
qualcuno	33	reale	52	richiesta	84
quale	3	realmente	96	ricominciare	96
quale	13	realtà	32	riconoscere	12
qualità	46	recente	31	ricordare	86
qualsiasi	56	recentemente	94	ricordo	24
qualunque	82	recevere	22	ridere	25
quando	4	reciproco	98	ridurre	41
quantità	64	reggere	97	riempire	63
quanto	16, 21, 34	regina	98	rientrare	66
quarto	89	regione	60	rifare	90
quasi	9, 19	regno	66	riferire	27
quattro	12	regola	71	riflettere	46
quella	2, 3	regolare	84	rigido	79
quello	2, 3	regolare	96	riguardare	28
questa	1, 6	relativo	67	riguardo	48
questione	29	relazione	29	rilevare	53
questo	1, 6	religione	95	rilievo	67
qui	8	religioso	39	rimanere	7
quindi	12	rendere	11	rimettere	58
raccogliere	17	reparto	100	ringraziare	65
raccolta	84	repubblica	61	rinnovare	80
raccomandare	71	resistenza	67	ripetere	19
raccontare	42	resistere	80	riportare	44
racconto	88	respingere	83	riposo	75
radio	79	respiro	73	riprendere	25
ragazza	63	responsabile	72	risalire	87
ragazzo	32	restare	13	risolvere	42
raggio	61	resto	17	rispetto	60
raggiungere	16	rete	66	rispondere	16
ragionare	70	retta	85	risposta	54
ragione	13	ricchezza	48	risultare	50
ramo	44	ricco	16	risultato	42
rapidamente	74	ricerca	53	risvegliare	99
rapido	45				

settimana	35	solco	97	spesa	70
severo	84	soldato	44	spesso	17
sezione	55	sole	13	spettacolo	45
sforzo	38	solenne	72	spiegare	29
sfruttare	96	solido	91	spiegazione	86
sfuggire	54	solito	56, 98	spingere	30
sguardo	42	sollevare	44	spirito	15
si	1	solo	7	spirituale	62
siccome	92	soluzione	51	splendore	72
sicuro	21	sonno	89	sposa	99
sicurrezza	58	sopra	11	sposare	60
significare	69	sopratutto	33	stabilire	40
significato	37	sorella	47	staccare	81
signora	19	sorgere	31	stagione	43
signore	16	sorprendere	78	stamattina	77
signorina	46	sorpresa	100	stampa	53
silenzio	30	sorridere	47	stanco	61
silenzioso	92	sorriso	68	stanza	43
simbolo	81	sospetto	67	stare	3
simile	23	sostanza	56	stasera	71
simpatia	99	sostare	94	stato	14
simpatico	87	sostenere	36	statua	85
sincero	92	sostituire	63	stazione	27
singolare	48	sottile	31	stella	34
singolo	83	sotto	6	stesso	6, 81
sinistra	93	spalla	34	stile	86
sinistro	99	sparare	99	storia	31
sino	59	spargere	87	storico	37
sistema	28	sparire	90	strada	14
situazione	36	spazio	69	straniero	60, 78
sociale	41	specchio	57	strano	35
società	21	speciale	28	straordinario	25
soffocare	88	specialmente	18	strappare	59
soffrire	37	specie	17, 79	stretto	38
soglia	84	spegnere	58	stringere	56
sogno	29	speranza	41	strumento	67
solamente	6	sperare	31		

studiare	30	tecnico	97	tradurre	97
studio	17	tedesco	58	tragic	73
studioso	54	telegramma	92	tranquillo	48
stupore	83	tema	50	trarre	21
su	2	temere	40	trascinare	56
sua	2	tempo	5, 89	trascorrere	90
subire	68	tendere	36	trascurare	84
subito	9, 96	tenere	7	trasformare	78
succedere	36	tenerezza	100	trattare	13
successo	38	tenero	78	trattato	58
sud	51	tensione	100	trattenere	70
suggerire	83	tentare	22	tratto	24
suo	2, 70	tentativo	79	tre	7
suolo	68	teoria	58	tremare	73
suonare	54	termine	33	treno	49
suono	47	terra	9	trenta	77
superare	44	terreno	42	trincea	78
superficie	81	terribile	52	triste	33
superiore	26	terzo	36, 94	tristezza	78
supporre	73	tesi	95	tronco	86
suscitare	96	tesoro	67	troppo	17, 30
svegliare	72	testa	16	trovare	4
sviluppare	76	tetto	97	tu	18
sviluppo	28	ti	7	tuo	20
svolgere	27	tipo	33	turbare	63
tacere	28	tirare	62	tutta	2
tagliare	48	titolo	68	tuttavia	32
tale	9, 37	toccare	22	tutti e due	28
talvolta	88	togliere	28	tutto	2, 21
Tanto	9, 20, 43	tomba	57	tuttora	72
tardi	28	tono	52	uccello	96
tavolo	23	tornare	10	uccidere	40
te	21	tra	5	ufficiale	72
tè	76	traccia	49	ufficio	28
teatro	43	tracciare	96	uguale	45, 92
tecnica	88	tradizione	61	ulteriore	96

ultimo	7, 94	verde	37	volare	70
umanità	44	vergogna	84	volentieri	86
umano	15	verità	18	volere	3
umido	74	vero	7	volgere	53
umile	65	verso	9, 93	volo	77
umore	94	veste	59	volontà	24
una	1	vestire	64	volta	4
unico	21	vestito	76, 82	volto	35
unione	88	vetro	92	volume	38
unire	74	vi	8	vostro	19
unità	64	via	8, 22	vuoto	56, 76
unito	76	viaggiatore	75	zio	77
università	40	viaggio	18	zona	38
universitario	91	vicenda	77		
uno	1, 6	vicinanza	98		
uomo	4	vicino	29, 40		
usare	31	villa	31		
uscire	9	villaggio	93		
uso	41	vincere	44		
utile	41	vino	58		
vago	78	violento	68		
valere	20	violenza	95		
valle	61	virtù	45		
valore	14	visione	88		
vano	100	visita	53		
vario	14	visitare	50		
vaso	95	viso	38		
vasto	27	vista	22		
ve	61	vita	5		
vecchio	8, 65	vittima	67		
vedere	3	vittoria	54		
velo	77	vivere	10		
velocità	78	vivo	13		
vendere	56	vizio	89		
venire	3	voce	13		
venti	47	voglia	85		
veramente	20	voi	18		

ENGLISH
INDEX

brown	69
build	38
building	71
bunch	80
bundle	80
burn	71
burning	99
but	2, 10
buy	69
by	1, 13
by now	16
by the way	32
by which	76
call	8
call back	47
calm	57, 73, 100
camp	14
campaign	29
can	2
canal	98
capable	59
capacious	59
capital	87
captain	97
card	29
care	28
carry	6
carry forward	44
cart	82
case	10, 94
cashier's desk	94
castle	70
cat	75
catch	5
category	73
Catholic	77
cause	31
cause	36
cease	67

celebrated	79
cemetery	74
central	52
centre	39
century	16
ceremony	94
certain	7
certainly	29, 39
certainty	64
chain	79
chair, seat	84
chamber	13
chambermaid	78
change	17, 35, 40
change round	84
channel	98
chapter	87
character	15, 50
characteristic	54
charge	80
charge	99
charity	66
charm	24
charming	64, 78
cheap	37
chest	63
chief	11
child	25, 53
choose	41
chorus	90
Christian	48
church	16
cinema	79
circle	39, 86
circulate	48
circumstance	64
cite	76
citizen	70
city	8

civil	52
civilisation	43
clarify	74
class	43
classic(al)	55
clean	86
clear	14, 86
clever	87
climb	15
clock	74
close	14
close by	40, 91
closed	28
cloud	94
coast	76
coat	42
coffee	62
cold	35, 79
collaboration	100
colleague	80
collect together	17
collection	84
college	75
colonel	75
colonial	77
colour	19
column	72
come	3
come out	10
comedy	45
comfort	44
comfortable	85
command	11, 55
Commander	52
commerce	53
commercial	83
commission	51
commit	78
committee	83

stir	99	Sunday	74	ten	25
stone	90	sunny	44	tender	78
stop	19, 66, 94	superior	26	tenderness	100
story	88	support	36, 97	tension	100
straight line	85	suppose	73	terminate	92
strange	35	supreme	26	terrible	52
stream	65	sure	7, 21	test	40
street	8, 14	surface	81	than	1
strength	10	surprise	78, 100	thank	65
stretch	36	surround	95	thanks	24
strict	38	surroundings	61	that	1, 2, 8
strike	66	suspect person	67	that is	12
string	80	suspicion	67	that one	3, 43
stroke	24	sustain	36	the	1
stroll	26	sweet	35	theatre	43
strong	18, 100	symbol	81	their	3
struggle	39	sympathy	99	them	6
study	17, 30	system	28	theme	36
style	86	table	23	then	4, 6, 13
subject	26, 50	take	5, 71	theory	58
substance	56	take away	28	there	10, 17, 24, 30, 89
substitute	63	take away	53	there is, are	23
subtle	31	take care	56	therefore	12, 22
succeed	10	talent	80	thesis	95
success	38	tall	8, 14	they	3, 9
such	9, 23, 37	tart	95	thick	23
sudden	43, 96	taste	46	thief	65
suddenly	9, 91	tea	76	thin	31
suffer	37, 68	teach	46	thing	4
suffice	17	teacher	14	think	7
sufficient	61	teaching	77	third	36, 94
sufficiently	95	tear away	59	thirty	77
suffocate	88	technical	97	this	1, 6, 8
suggest	83	technique	88	this morning	77
suit	39, 76	tediously	69	thought	11
suitable	50	telegram	92	thousand	69, 93
summer	53	tell	42	thread	47
summons	81	temporary	96	three	7
sun	13	tempt	22	threshold	84

throat	100	traveller	75	us	3
through	1, 17	treasure	67	use	31, 41, 74
throw	46, 58, 60	treasury	67	useful	41
thus	4	treaty	58	useless	44
ticket	69	tree	33	usual	56, 98
tied	90	tremble	73	vain	100
time	4, 5, 89	trench	78	valley	61
tip	81	trial	59, 97	value	14
tired	61	trouble	29, 46, 63	van	82
title	68	true	7	various	12, 14
to	1	trunk	86	vase	95
to her	6	trust	69	vast	27
to it	3	truth	18	vault	98
to me	5	try	9, 40	veil	77
to them	6	turn	4, 26, 53, 77, 84	verse	93
to you	8, 21, 61	turn (over)	34	very	7, 2126, 29
today	8	turn round	48	very much	27, 59
together	14	tutor	36	vice	89
tomb	57, 98	twenty	47	victim	67
tomorrow	55	two	3, 28	victory	54
tone	52	type	33	view	22
tongue	27	ugly	47	vigorous	49
tonight	71	ulterior	96	villa	31
too	2	uncertain	100	village	11, 93
too much	17, 30	uncle	77	violence	95
tooth	50	under	6	violent	68
top	39, 64	undergo	68	virtue	45
touch	22	understand	13, 14, 16	vision	88
towards	9, 99	unfold	27	visit	50, 53
town	11	union	88	voice	13
trace	49, 96	unit	64	void	76
trace back	87	united	76	volume	38
track	49	unity	64	wait	14
tradition	61	university	40	wait for	25
tragic	73	unknown	100	waitress	78
train	49	until	12, 20, 52, 59	waiving	84
transform	78	up there	71	wake (of ship)	97
translate	97	upon	2, 11	wake up	72
travel	66	urge	98	walk	41

SPANISH KEY WORDS

The basic 2,000-word vocabulary
arranged by frequency in a
hundred units.

With comprehensive Spanish and
English indexes.

PEDRO CASAL

The Oleander Press

The Oleander Press
16 Orchard Street
Cambridge
CB1 1JT
www.oleanderpress.com

CONTENTS

Introduction

Spanish Key Words provides an easy route to mastering excellent basic Spanish. The 100-unit structure provides you with the most useful words quickly and easily, each unit consisting of 20 common words. These are the essential foundation stones on which you intuitively build your language framework. Computer analysis of a corpus of a million words has provided this essential list of the commonest two thousand key words in Spanish, with their meanings in English, arranged in decreasing order of frequency.

The first five units (100 words) account for 50% of conversational Spanish; the first 500 words account for 75% of normal usage; the full 2,000 will equip you for nearly all word occurrences of modern Spanish usage in speech, newspapers, books, television, internet etc. It also provides an all-in-one basic Spanish-English dictionary and an all-in-one basic English-Spanish dictionary.

Spanish Key Words is the perfect fast, easy aid to learning Spanish by using the simplest, most logical way to pick up a vocabulary of ten thousand words from just two thousand.

The Units

Each of the hundred units is self-contained, Unit 1 including the twenty commonest key words, Unit 2 the next commonest and so on. The key word is followed by an indication of its part of speech: *adj.*, adjective; *adv.*, adverb; *conj.*, conjunction, *f.n.*, feminine noun; *interj.*, interjection; *m.n.*, masculine noun; *num.*, numeral; *prep.*, preposition; *pron.*, pronoun. Verbs are not so shown, because they are represented in each instance by their infinitive, which is always translated beginning with 'to'.

Masculine nouns and adjectives form their feminine by changing their final vowel from *o* to *a*, unless otherwise shown. So masculine *amarillo* becomes feminine *amarilla*.

Singular nouns and adjectives form their plural by adding *s* if ending in a vowel, or *es* if ending in a consonant, unless otherwise shown. So singular *amarillo* becomes plural *amarillos* and singular *amarilla* becomes *amarillas*. So singular *lugar* becomes plural *lugares*.

Regular verbs ending in *ar*, *-er* and *-ir* are conjugated in model form in a separate table just before the hundred units. The commonest irregular verbs are conjugated (with pronouns and meanings in the early units) in the present tense of the active voice, indicative mood, wherever their infinitive occurs in order of frequency. Though verbs appear only in their infinitive form, their position in the units has been calculated from the total occurrence of all their parts.

Many Spanish words may be translated by a number of English equivalents. It would be counter-productive, in a work designed to stimulate interest rather than to clog the memory, to list all such equivalents, so only the most common have been cited, with the commonest of all first. When consulting the two indexes, therefore, the reader who cannot find a given word should try to think of synonyms or near-synonyms if a certain word seems to be omitted.

Regular Verbs
in the Present Tense

First Conjugation   Cantar,   to sing

yo canto	I sing	nosotros cantamos	we sing
tú cantas	you (s.) sing	vosotros cantais	you (pl.) sing
él canta	he sings	ellos cantan	they sing

Second Conjugation   Temer,   to fear

yo temo	I fear	nosotros tememos	we fear
tú tomes	you (s.) fear	vosotros teméis	you (pl.) fear
él teme	he fears	ellos temen	they fear

Third Conjugation   Partir,   to leave, depart

yo parto	I leave	nosotros partimos	we leave
tú partes	you (s.) leave	vosotros partis	you (pl.) leave
él parte	he leaves	ellos parten	they leave

N .B. Conventionally, 'él', 'he' stands also for 'ella', 'she' in the conjugation of the present tense throughout this frequency list.

155

SPANISH KEYWORDS

Unit 1

de *(prep.)* — of
el *(m., pl. los - art.)* — the
la *(f. pl. las - art.)* — the
y *(conj.)* — and
a *(prep.)* — to, at
en *(prep.)* — in, into
él *(pron.)* — he

ser — to be, being
   yo soy — I am
   tú eres — you *(s.)* are
   él es — he is
   nosotros somos — we are
   vosotros sois — you *(pl.)* are
   ellos son — they are

que *(pron.)* — that, which, who, what

haber — to have
   yo he — I have
   tú has — you *(s.)* have
   él ha — he has
   nosotros habemos — we have
   vosotros habéis — you *(pl.)* have
   ellos han — they have

que *(conj.)* — that
su *(adj.)* — his, hers, its, your, their
no *(adv.)* — not
un *(m. - art.)* — a, an
por *(prep.)* — by, through
con *(prep.)* — with
una *(f. - art.)* — a, an
yo *(pron.)* — I

estar — to be
   yo estoy — I am
   tú estás — you *(s.)* are
   él está — he is
   nosotros estamos — we are
   vosotros estáis — you *(pl.)* are
   ellos están — they are

tener — to have
   yo tengo — I have
   tú tienes — you *(s.)* have
   él tiene — he has
   nosotros tenemos — we have
   vosotros tenéis — you *(pl.)* have
   ellos tienen — they have

Unit 2

ella *(pron.)*	she
para *(prep.)*	for
este *(adj.)*	this
lo *(art.)*	it
más *(adv.)*	more
como *(conj.)*	as, how
ello *(pron.)*	it
ir	to go
yo voy I go	nosotros vamos we go
tú vas you *(s.)* go	vosotros vais you *(pl.)* go
él va he goes	ellos van they go
decir	to say
yo digo I say	nosotros decimos we say
tú dices you *(s.)* say	vosotros decís you *(pl.)* say
él dice he says	ellos dicen they say
todo *(adj.)*	all, every, whole
tú *(pron.)*	you *(s., informal)*
pero *(conj.)*	but, yet
hacer	to do, make
yo hago I do	nosotros hacemos we make
tú haces you *(s.)* do	vosotros hacéis you *(pl.)* make
él hace he does	ellos hacen they make
poder	to be able
yo puedo I can	nosotros podemos we can
tú puedes you *(s.)* can	vosotros podéis you *(pl.)* can
él puede he can	ellos pueden they can
usted *(pron.)*	you *(s. formal)*
o *(conj.)*	either, or
ya *(adv.)*	already
otro *(adj.)*	another, other
mi *(adj.)*	my

Unit 3

ver	to see
yo veo	nosotros vemos
tú ves	vosotros veis
él ve	ellos ven
dar	to give
yo doy	nosotros damos
tú das	vosotros dais
él da	ellos dan
sin *(prep.)*	without
ese *(adj.)*	that
querer	to want
yo quiero	nosotros queremos
tú quieres	vosotros queréis
él quiere	ellos quieren
dos *(num.)*	two
hombre *(m.n.)*	man
nuestro *(adj.)*	our, ours
sobre *(pron.)*	on, above, about
porque *(conj.)*	because
cuándo *(adv.)*	when
mismo *(adj.)*	same
grande *(adj.)*	large, great
muy *(adv.)*	very
vida *(f.n.)*	life
vez *(f.n.)*	time, occassion
saber	to know
yo sé	nosotros sabemos
tú sabes	vosotros sabéis
él sabe	ellos saben
eso *(pron.)*	that
primer *(adj.)*	first
aquel *(adj.)*	that

Unit 4

entre *(prep.)*	between, among
día *(m.n.)*	day
don *(m.n.)*	Mr
sí *(adv.)*	yes
tan *(adv.)*	so
todo *(pron.)*	all, everything
también *(adv.)*	too, also
pues *(conj.)*	well, then
hasta *(pron.)*	until
algún *(adj.)*	any, some
año *(m.n.)*	year
aquí *(adv.)*	here
ni *(conj.)*	neither, nor
uno *(num.)*	one
pasar	to pass
venir	to come
yo vengo	nosotros venimos
tú vienes	vosotros venís
él viene	ellos vienen
señor *(m.n.)*	Mr, gentleman
cómo *(adv.)*	how? Why?
mujer *(f.n.)*	woman, wife
llegar	to arrive

creer	to believe
bien *(adv.)*	well
siempre *(adv.)*	always
mucho *(adj.)*	a lot of, much
casa *(f.n.)*	house
parecer	to seem
yo parezco	nosotros parecemos
tú pareces	vosotros parecéis
él parece	ellos parecen
ahora *(adv.)*	now
cosa *(f.n.)*	thing
hablar	to speak
deber	to have to, owe
dejar	to leave
así *(adv.)*	thus, so
dónde *(adv.)*	where?
tiempo *(m.n.)*	time
sólo *(adv.)*	only
tres *(num.)*	three
desde *(prep.)*	from, since
bueno *(adj.)*	good
parte *(f.n.)*	part
esto *(pron.)*	this

Unit 6

llevar	to bear, carry
mil *(adj. Num.)*	thousand
ciento *(adj. Num.)*	hundred
después *(adv.)*	afterwards
mundo *(m.n.)*	world
llamar	to knock, call (llamarse, to be called)
sino *(conj.)*	except, but (after negative)
poner	to put
yo pongo	nosotros ponemos
tú pones	vosotros ponéis
él pone	ellos ponen
vivir	to live
cual *(pron.)*	which, who, whom
obra *(f.n.)*	work
quedar	to remain
español *(adj.)*	Spanish
encontrar	to meet
pensar	to think
salir	to go out, leave
yo salgo	nosotros salimos
tú sales	vosotros salís
él sale	ellos salen
volver	to return
yo vuelvo	nosotros volvemos
tú vuelves	vosotros volvéis
él vuelve	ellos vuelven
pueblo *(m.n.)*	people, village
nuevo *(adj.)*	new
cada *(adj.)*	each

seguir	to follow
yo sigo	nosotros seguimos
tú sigues	vosotros seguís
él sigue	ellos siguen
quien *(pron.)*	who
antes *(adv.)*	before
conocer	to be acquainted with
yo conozco	nosotros conocemos
tú conoces	vosotros conocéis
él conoce	ellos conocen
aun *(adv.)*	even
tu *(adj.)*	your
mirar	to look at
verdad *(f.n.)*	truth
poco *(adj.)*	little, slight
tal *(adj.)*	such
señora *(f.n.)*	Mrs, lady
ciudad *(f.n.)*	city
oír	to hear, listen to
yo oigo	nosotros oímos
tú oyes	vosotros oís
él oye	ellos oyen
mano *(f.n.)*	hand
éste *(pron.)*	this
dios *(m.n.)*	god
hoy *(adv.)*	today
hora *(f.n.)*	hour
libro *(m.n.)*	book
historia *(f.n.)*	history

Unit 8

sentir	to feel, be sorry, hear
yo siento	nosotros sentimos
tú sientes	vosotros sentís
él siente	ellos sienten
ojo *(m.n.)*	eye
momento *(m.n.)*	moment
cierto *(adj.)*	certain, correct
menos *(adv.)*	less
cinco *(num.)*	five
palabra *(f.n.)*	word
caso *(m.n.)*	case, notice
nada *(pron.)*	nothing
siglo *(m.n.)*	century
hijo *(m.n.)*	son
último *(adj)*	last
padre *(m.n.)*	father
noche *(f.n.)*	night
casi *(adv.)*	nearly
idea *(f.n.)*	idea
punto *(m.n.)*	point
entrar	to enter
nunca *(adv.)*	never
entonces *(adv.)*	then

Unit 9

tanto *(adj.)*	so much, so many
tomar	to take
estado *(m.n.)*	state
décimo *(adj.)*	tenth
modo *(m.n.)*	way, method
escribir	to write
cuanto *(adj.)*	how much, how many
mucho *(adv.)*	a great deal, much
acabar	to have just, finish, end
luz *(f.n.)*	light
uno *(pron.)*	one
trabajo *(m.n.)*	work
luego *(adv.)*	then, later, next
tierra *(f.n.)*	land, earth
nombre *(m.n.)*	name
mayor *(adj.)*	greater, major, elder, oldest
calle *(f.n.)*	street
nadie *(pron.)*	nobody
aunque *(conj.)*	though, although
fin *(m.n.)*	end

Unit 10

amor *(m.n.)*	love
propio *(adj.)*	own
autor *(m.n.)*	author
ése *(pron.)*	that (one)
nada *(adv.)*	in no way
país *(m.n.)*	country
cuatro *(num.)*	four
esperar	to wait, hope, expect
otro *(pron.)*	other, another
madre *(f.n.)*	mother
amigo *(m.n.)*	friend
espíritu *(m.n.)*	spirit
grupo *(m.n.)*	group
ciencia *(f.n.)*	science
aparecer	to appear, seem
yo aparezco	nosotros aparecemos
tú apareces	vosotros aparecéis
él aparece	ellos aparecen
contar	to count, tell
yo cuento	nosotros contamos
tú cuentas	vosotros contáis
él cuenta	ellos cuentan
servir	to serve
yo sirvo	nosotros servimos
tú sirves	vosotros servís
él sirve	ellos sirven
ninguno *(adj.)*	no, nobody
ante *(prep.)*	before, in the presence of
perder	to lose
yo pierdo	nosotros perdemos
tú pierdes	vosotros perdéis
él pierde	ellos pierden

cultura *(f.n.)*	culture
forma *(f.n.)*	form
arte *(m.n.) (s.)*	art
artes *(f.n.) (pl.)*	
ésta *(pron.)*	this (one)
solo *(adj.)*	single, sole
quién *(pron.)*	who?
claro *(adj.)*	clear, bright, light
más *(adj.)*	more
tratar	to treat, handle
estudio *(m.n.)*	study
hacia *(prep.)*	towards
seis *(num.)*	six
medio *(adj.)*	half, average
razón *(f.n.)*	reason, ratio
lugar *(m.n.)*	place
buscar	to seek
camino *(m.n.)*	way, road
realidad *(f.n.)*	reality
mañana *(f.n.)*	morning, tomorrow
fuerza *(f.n.)*	strenght, force, power

alto *(adj.)*	high, tall
formar	to form
durante *(adv.)*	during
traer	to bring, carry
yo traigo	nosotros traemos
tú traes	vosotros traéis
él trae	ellos traen
cuando *(conj.)*	when
mejor *(adj.)*	better
allí *(adv.)*	there
guerra *(f.n.)*	war
leer	to read
yo leo	nosotros leemos
tú lees	vosotros leéis
él lee	ellos leen
ocho *(num.)*	eight
hallar	to find
gobierno *(m.n.)*	government
gracia *(f.n.)*	grace, kindness, wit (pl. thanks)
carácter *(m.n.)*	character
época *(f.n.)*	period
dentro *(adv.)*	inside
contra *(prep.)*	against
lado *(m.n.)*	side
bajo *(adv.)*	down, below
tarde *(f.n.)*	afternoon

persona *(f.n.)*	person
empezar	to begin
yo empiezo	nosotros empezamos
tú empieces	vosotros empezáis
él empiece	ellos empiezan
presentar	to present
vario *(adj.)*	varied, variable
malo *(adj.)*	bad, wretched, unpleasant
gente *(f.n.)*	people
problema *(m.n.)*	problem
hija *(f.n.)*	daughter
antiguo *(adj.)*	ancient, old
nueve *(num.)*	nine
mes *(m.n.)*	month
alma *(f.n.)*	soul, spirit
dicho *(adj.)*	said, above-mentioned
color *(m.n.)*	colour
todavía *(adv.)*	still, yet
hecho *(m.n.)*	deed, act, fact
número *(m.n.)*	number
cuerpo *(m.n.)*	body
según *(prep.)*	according to
morir	to die
yo muero	nosotros morimos
tú mueres	vosotros morís
él muere	ellos mueren

vaso *(m.n.)*	glass
general *(adj.)*	general
pedir	to ask for
yo pido	nosotros pedimos
tú pides	vosotros pedís
él pide	ellos piden
gustar	to please ('me gusta', 'it pleases me', 'I like')
poco *(adv.)*	little, not much
además *(adv.)*	moreover
faltar	to lack
niño *(m.n.)*	boy, child
novela *(f.n.)*	novel
recibir	to receive
corazón *(m.n.)*	heart
andar	to go
tipo *(m.n.)*	type
segundo *(adj.)*	second
caer	to fall
yo caigo	nosotros caemos
tú caes	vosotros caéis
él cae	ellos caen
viejo *(adj.)*	old
comprender	to understand
sentido *(m.n.)*	meaning

Unit 15

algo *(pron.)*	anything, something
igual *(adj.)*	equal
humano *(adj.)*	human
campo *(m.n.)*	field, country(side)
pequeño *(adj.)*	small
elemento *(m.n.)*	element
exister	to exist
clase *(f.n.)*	class(room)
puerta *(f.n.)*	door(way), gate(way)
ocurrir	yo occur
cuyo *(pron.)*	whose, of which
relación *(f.n.)*	relation(ship)
necesitar	to need
poeta *(m.n., f.n.)* (also *f.n.* poetisa)	poet
valor *(m.n.)*	value, courage
político *(adj.)*	political
producir	to produce
posible *(adj.)*	possible
tanto *(adv.)*	as much, so much
recordar	to remember, remind

Unit 16

línea *(f.n.)*	line
objeto *(m.n.)*	object
ahí *(adv.)*	there
cabeza *(f.n.)*	head
aire *(m.n.)*	air
pronto *(adv.)*	quickly, early
ejemplo *(m.n.)*	example
doña *(f.n.)*	Mrs
doctor *(m.n.)*	doctor
mar *(m.n.)*	sea
blanco *(adj.)*	white
largo *(adj.)*	long
pobre *(adj.)*	poor
península *(f.n.)*	peninsula
comenzar	to begin
yo comienzo	nosotros comenzamos
tú comienzas	vosotros comenzáis
él comienza	ellos comienzan
siguiente *(adj.)*	following
callar	to be quiet
embargo *(m.n.)*	embargo, seizure ('sin embargo', 'however')
cuenta *(f.n.)*	account
explicar	to explain

Unit 17

cuya *(pron.)*	whose, of which
región *(f.n.)*	region
referir	to refer
yo refiero	nosotros referimos
tú refieres	vosotros referís
él refiere	ellos refieren
preguntar	to ask
verdadero *(adj.)*	true, truthful, real
maestro *(m.n.)*	master, teacher
interés *(m.n.)*	interest
efecto *(m.n.)*	effect
fondo *(m.n.)*	back(ground), bottom, fund
español *(m.n.)*	Spaniard (male)
natural *(adj.)*	natural
pie *(m.n.)*	feet
ofrecer	to offer
yo ofrezco	nosotros ofrecemos
tú ofreces	vosotros ofrecéis
él ofrece	ellos ofrecen
medio *(m.n.)*	middle, medium
noticia *(f.n.)*	notice, *(pl.)* news
república *(f.n.)*	republic
manera *(f.n.)*	way, manner
considerar	to consider
abrir	to open
único *(adj.)*	only, unique

correr	to run
voz *(f.n.)*	voice
pensamiento *(m.n.)*	thought
acción *(f.n.)*	action
por qué *(adv.)*	why
estudiar	to study
duda *(f.n.)*	doubt
frente *(m.n.)*	front, face
social *(adj.)*	social
real *(adj.)*	royal, real
público *(adj.)*	public
imagen *(f.n.)*	image, picture
crear	to create
conseguir	to get, bring about
yo consigo	nosotros conseguimos
tú consigues	vosotros conseguís
él consigue	ellos consiguen
distinto *(adj.)*	distinct, different
soler (+ infinitive)	to be in the habit of
yo suelo	nosotros solemos
tú sueles	vosotros soléis
él suele	ellos suelen
francés *(adj.)*	French
caballero *(m.n.)*	gentleman, rider
sol *(m.n.)*	sun
siete *(num.)*	seven

rey *(m.n.)*	king
familia *(f.n.)*	family
entender	to understand
yo entiendo	nosotros entendemos
tú entiendes	vosotros entendéis
él entiende	ellos entienden
olvidar	to forget
paso *(m.n.)*	step, passage, walk
dinero *(m.n.)*	money
publicar	to publish
algo *(adv.)*	rather, a bit
lleno *(adj.)*	full
ocupar	to occupy, employ
preciso *(adj.)*	necessary, exact
muerte *(f.n.)*	death
nacional *(adj.)*	national
cambio *(m.n.)*	exchange, change
resultar	to result
principio *(m.n.)*	beginning, principle
tampoco *(adv.)*	neither
centro *(m.n.)*	centre
marchar	to go, function, march
río *(m.n.)*	river

causa *(f.n.)*	cause
cara *(f.n.)*	face, appearance
cielo *(m.n.)*	sky, heaven
levantar	to raise (up)
condición *(f.n.)*	condition
brazo *(m.n.)*	arm
quizá(s) *(adv.)*	perhaps
dormir	to sleep
duermo	dormimos
duermes	dormís
duerme	duermen
descripción *(f.n.)*	description
anterior *(adj.)*	former, previous, front
nacer	to be born
nazco	nacemos
naces	nacéis
nace	nacen
mientras *(adv.)*	(mean)while
sacar	to get out, extract
marido *(m.n.)*	husband
echar	to throw, cast
permitir	to permit
literario *(adj.)*	literary
ministro *(m.n.)*	minister
trabajar	to work
suelo *(m.n.)*	ground, floor

Unit 21

detener	to delay, hold up
detengo	detenemos
detienes	detenéis
detiene	detienen
viaje *(m.n.)*	journey, trip
treinta *(num.)*	thirty
lejos *(adv.)*	far away
joven (m.n., f.n.)	young man, young woman
partido *(m.n.)*	party, match
casar	to marry
poco (un) *(m.n.)*	(a) little
representar	to represent, perform
universidad *(f.n.)*	university
derecho *(m.n.)*	law, right, duty, straight
carta *(f.n.)*	card, letter
origen *(m.n.)*	origin
suponer	to suppose
supongo	suponemos
supones	suponéis
supone	suponen
edad *(f.n.)*	age
papel *(m.n.)*	paper, role
negro *(adj.)*	black
falta *(f.n.)*	lack, failure, fault
médico *(m.n.)*	doctor
ganar	to earn, gain, win

hermano *(m.n.)*	brother
movimiento *(m.n.)*	movement
escuela *(f.n.)*	school
científico *(adj.)*	scientific
moderno *(adj.)*	modern
otra *(pron.)*	(an)other *(f.)*
término *(m.n.)*	end, boundary, term
puro *(adj.)*	pure
figura *(f.n.)*	figure
método *(m.n.)*	method
ayer *(adv.)*	yesterday
actual *(adj.)*	present, current
general *(m.n.)*	general
sentimiento *(m.n.)*	feeling, emotion
continuar	to continue
motivo *(m.n.)*	reason, motive
gusto *(m.n.)*	taste, pleasure
comer	to eat
repetir	to repeat
repito	repetimos
repites	repetís
repite	repiten
zona *(f.n.)*	zone

Unit 23

¡ay! *(int.)*	oh!
mismo *(pron.)*	self (' yo mismo ', 'I myself')
poder *(m.n.)*	power
ésa *(pron.)*	that (one), the former (f.)
función *(f.n.)*	function, performance
ocasión *(f.n.)*	occasion
convenir	to agree, be good for
convengo	convenimos
convienes	convenís
conviene	convienen
sentar	to sit, settle
siento	sentamos
sientas	sentáis
sienta	sientan
terminar	to complete, stop
próximo *(adj.)*	near, next
sociedad *(f.n.)*	society
cuestión *(f.n.)*	matter, quarrel
valer	to be worth(y), equal, protect
allá *(adv.)*	there
flor *(f.n.)*	flower
oro *(m.n.)*	gold
diez *(num.)*	ten
provincia *(f.n.)*	province
tocar	to play, touch, concern
demostrar	to demonstrate, to show
demuestro	demostramos
demuestras	demostráis
demuestra	demuestran

Unit 24

lector *(m.n.)*	reader
televisión *(f.n.)*	television
mandar	to order, send, be in command
rico *(adj.)*	rich
hermana *(f.n.)*	sister
acto *(m.n.)*	act(ion), deed
señorita *(f.n.)*	miss, young lady
servicio *(m.n.)*	service
bastar	to suffice
difícil *(adj.)*	difficult
histórico *(adj.)*	historic(al)
desear	to desire
profundo *(adj.)*	deep
conocido *(adj.)*	(well-)known
fuera *(adv.)*	out(side), away
escritor *(m.n.)*	writer
llorar	to weep
política *(f.n.)*	politics
reconocer	to recognise
reconozco	reconocemos
reconoces	reconocéis
reconoce	reconocen
opinión *(f.n.)*	opinion

Unit 25

libre *(adj.)*	free
mostrar	to show
muestro	mostramos
muestras	mostráis
muestra	muestran
artículo *(m.n.)*	article
importancia *(f.n.)*	importance
revolución *(f.n.)*	revolution
matar	to kill
¡ah! *(int.)*	ah!
suceder	to happen, succeed
cambiar	to (ex)change
feliz *(adj.)*	happy
sufrir	to suffer
constituir	to constitute
constituyo	constituimos
constituyes	constituís
constituye	constituyen
llamado *(adj.)*	called
iglesia *(f.n.)*	church
poseer	to possess
hotel *(m.n.)*	hotel
triste *(adj.)*	sad
conocimiento *(m.n.)*	knowledge, acquaintance
celebrar	to celebrate
geografía *(f.n.)*	geography

pesar	to weigh
valle *(m.n.)*	valley
autoridad *(f.n.)*	authority
añadir	to add
conservar	to preserve, keep
posición *(f.n.)*	position
defender	to defend
defiendo	defendemos
defiendes	defendéis
defiende	defienden
niña *(f.n.)*	girl, child (f.)
concepto *(m.n.)*	concept(ion)
demás *(pron.)*	rest, others
importante *(adj.)*	important
principal *(adj.)*	principal
fijar	to fix
propósito *(m.n.)*	purpose, intention
piedra *(f.n.)*	stone
situación *(f.n.)*	situation
una *(pron.)*	somebody (f.)
necesario *(adj.)*	necessary
serie *(f.n.)*	series
mal *(adv.)*	badly

observar	to observe
cuarto *(m.n.)*	room, quarter
sistema *(m.n.)*	system
hecho *(adj.)*	complete, done
aspecto *(m.n.)*	appearance, aspect
sombra *(f.n.)*	shade, shadow
adquirir	to acquire
adquiero	adquirimos
adquieres	adquirís
adquiere	adquieren
especie *(f.n.)*	species
población *(f.n.)*	population, hamlet
boca *(f.n.)*	mouth
tercero *(adj.)*	third
personaje *(m.n.)*	celebrity, character
cualquier *(pron.)*	anybody, whichever
subir	to raise, go up, climb
ambos *(adj.)*	both
recoger	to gather, pick up
recojo	recogemos
recoges	recogéis
recoge	recogen
mesa *(f.n.)*	table
paz *(f.n.)*	peace
pasado *(adj.)*	past
minuto *(m.n.)*	minute

Unit 28

dirigir	to direct, manage, drive
dirijo	dirigimos
diriges	dirigís
dirige	dirigen
reír	to laugh
río	reímos
ríes	reís
ríe	ríen
completo *(adj.)*	complete, inclusive, full
proponer	to propose
propongo	proponemos
propones	proponéis
propone	proponen
importar	to be important, amount to, import
teatro *(m.n.)*	theatre
asunto *(m.n.)*	matter, subject
capítulo *(m.n.)*	chapter
existencia *(f.n.)*	existence
etcétera *(adv.)*	and so on
figurar	to figure, represent
meter	to put, place
aspecto *(m.n.)*	appearance, aspect
destino *(m.n.)*	destiny, destination
interesar	to interest
necesidad *(f.n.)*	need
diverso *(adj.)*	different, several
advertir	to notice, point out
advierto	advertimos
adviertes	advertís
advierte	advierten
plaza *(f.n.)*	square, place, job
literatura *(f.n.)*	literature

indicar	to indicate
periódico *(m.n.)*	journal
investigación *(f.n.)*	investigation
afirmar	to state, make steady
extraordinario *(adj.)*	extraordinary
pagar	to pay
lograr	to obtain, achieve
especial *(adj.)*	(e)special
capital *(m.n.)*	capital
nación *(f.n.)*	nation
veinte *(num.)*	twenty
popular *(adj.)*	popular
emplear	to employ, use
quitar	to take off, take away
artista (m.n., f.n.)	artist
pretender	to try to, claim
hermoso *(adj.)*	beautiful, handsome
cerca *(adv.)*	nearby
frase *(f.n.)*	sentence, quotation
escuchar	to listen (to)

árbol *(m.n.)*	tree
libertad *(f.n.)*	freedom
corresponder	to correspond, belong
acercar	to bring near
ventana *(f.n.)*	window
deseo *(m.n.)*	wish, desire
página *(f.n.)*	page
azul *(adj.)*	blue
acudir	to come (along), (up)
dirección *(f.n.)*	address, direction
estación *(f.n.)*	station, season
honor *(m.n.)*	honour
raro *(adj.)*	rare
exponer	to expose, expound, exhibit
expongo	exponemos
expones	exponéis
expone	exponen
acaso *(adv.)*	perhaps
precisamente	precisely
consistir	to consist
memoria *(f.n.)*	memory, report
descubrir	to discover
describir	to describe

acompañar	to accompany
cantar	to singer
comprar	to buy
común *(adj.)*	common
ser *(m.n.)*	being
bajar	to lower, bring down
religioso *(adj.)*	religious
reino *(m.n.)*	kingdom
norte *(m.n.)*	north
perdonar	to excuse, pardon
dolor *(m.n.)*	sorrow, pain
intelectual *(m.n.)*	intellectual
obrero *(m.n.)*	worker, labourer
naturaleza *(f.n.)*	nature
bello *(adj.)*	beautiful
visitar	to visit
cumplir	to carry out, fulfil
secreto *(m.n.)*	secret
guardar	to guard, keep
sangre *(m.n.)*	blood

masa *(f.n.)*	mass
apenas *(adv.)*	hardly
silencio *(m.n.)*	silence
millón *(m.n.)*	million
voluntad *(f.n.)*	will
esfuerzo *(m.n.)*	effort
favor *(m.n.)*	favour, service ('por favor', 'please')
intentar	to attempt, intend
alcanzar	to catch (up) (with), manage
círculo *(m.n.)*	circle
aparato *(m.n.)*	apparatus
superior *(adj.)*	upper, higher, superior
decidir	to decide
atención *(f.n.)*	attention
según *(adv.)*	it depends
conciencia *(f.n.)*	conscience
extraño *(adj.)*	strange
muchacha *(f.n.)*	girl
público *(m.n.)*	public
mantener	to maintain
mantengo	mantenemos
mantienes	mantenéis
mantiene	mantienen

discurso *(m.n.)*	speech, passage
toro *(m.n.)*	bull
juventud *(f.n.)*	youth
pasión *(f.n.)*	passion
técnica *(f.n.)*	technique, technology
disponer	to dispose, prepare
dispongo	disponemos
dispones	disponéis
dispone	disponen
instrumento *(m.n.)*	instrument
emoción *(f.n.)*	emotion
costa *(f.n.)*	coast, cost
fiesta *(f.n.)*	party, feast, festival
costumbre *(f.n.)*	custom, habit
merecer	to deserve
merezco	merecemos
mereces	merecéis
merece	merecen
mirada *(f.n.)*	glance, look
prueba *(f.n.)*	proof, test
nervioso *(adj.)*	nervous
suerte *(f.n.)*	luck
significar	to mean
espectáculo *(m.n.)*	spectacle, show
corriente *(f.n.)*	current
vivo *(adj.)*	living, lively

aceptar	to accept
fuego *(m.n.)*	fire
asegurar	to assure
interesante *(adj.)*	interesting
fuerte *(adj.)*	strong
observación *(f.n.)*	observation
coche *(m.n.)*	car, coach
simple *(adj.)*	simple
alguno *(pron.)*	some(one)
grave *(adj.)*	heavy, serious
género *(m.n.)*	class, genre, gender
notar	to note
seguro *(adj.)*	sure
justicia *(f.n.)*	justice
texto *(m.n.)*	text
aquél *(pron.)*	that (one)
objetivo *(m.n.)*	objective
grado *(m.n.)*	degree, step
recuerdo *(m.n.)*	memory, souvenir
obtener	to obtain
obtengo	obtenemos
obtienes	obtenéis
obtiene	obtienen

numeroso *(adj.)*	numerous
palacio *(m.n.)*	palace
contestar	to answer
tema *(m.n.)*	theme
alegría *(f.n.)*	happiness
asistir	to be present, attend
régimen *(m.n.)*	diet, régime
encima *(adv.)*	on top, above
puesto *(adj.)*	(clothes) wearing, (table) laid
miedo *(m.n.)*	fear
gloria *(f.n.)*	glory
letra *(f.n.)*	letter
mover	to move
muevo	movemos
mueves	movéis
mueve	mueven
militar *(adj.)*	military
vender	to sell
árabe *(adj.)*	Arab, Arabic
título *(m.n.)*	title
colocar	to place, put
responder	to reply
consejo *(m.n.)*	advice

Unit 36

bueno *(adj.)*	good
instante *(m.n.)*	instant
inglés *(adj.)*	English
menor *(adj.)*	minor, smaller, smallest, less, least
civil *(adj.)*	civil
nota *(f.n.)*	note, mark
jardín *(m.n.)*	garden
peseta *(f.n.)*	peseta
consecuencia *(f.n.)*	consequence
semana *(f.n.)*	week
sueño *(m.n.)*	sleep, dream
enseñar	to teach, train, show
ambiente *(m.n.)*	environment, atmosphere
labor *(f.n.)*	work, job
teoría *(f.n.)*	theory
cerrar	to close
cierro	cerramos
cierras	cerráis
cierra	cierran
asimismo *(adv.)*	in the same way
cuidado *(m.n.)*	care
respecto *(m.n.)*	respect
compañero *(m.n.)*	companion, mate

fácil *(adj.)*	easy
héroe *(m.n.)*	hero
ligero *(m.n.)*	light
balcón *(m.n.)*	balcony
lucha *(f.n.)*	struggle
experiencia *(f.n.)*	experience, experiment
señalar	to mark, point (out), (to)
influencia *(f.n.)*	influence
convertir	to convert
convierto	convertimos
conviertes	convertís
convierte	convierten
ejército *(m.n.)*	army
huir	to flee
huyo	huimos
huyes	huís
huye	huyen
manifestación *(f.n.)*	sign, declaration, rally
través *(m.n.)*	bend, bias, reverse
preparar	to prepare
actividad *(f.n.)*	activity
rato *(m.n.)*	while, period
contemplar	to contemplate
quince *(num.)*	fifteen
tarde *(adv.)*	late
enorme *(adj.)*	enormous

duro *(adj.)*	hard
enemigo *(m.n.)*	enemy
organización *(f.n.)*	organization
partir	set off, start, split (open)
jefe (m.n., f.n.)	chief, head
resultado *(m.n.)*	result
perfecto *(adj.)*	perfect
reducir	to reduce
reduzco	reducimos
reduces	reducís
reduce	reducen
dama *(f.n.)*	lady
bajo *(adj.)*	low, short
negar	to deny, refuse
niego	negamos
niegas	negáis
niega	niegan
juzgar	to judge
curva *(f.n.)*	curve
imponer	to impose
impongo	imponemos
impones	imponéis
impone	imponen
aprendar	to learn
demás *(adj.)*	other, rest (of them)
uso *(m.n.)*	use
plano *(m.n.)*	plan, plane
cuento *(m.n.)*	story
¡ja! (interj.)	ha!

jugar	to play
juego	jugamos
juegas	jugáis
juega	juegan
demasiado *(adj.)*	too
mejor *(adv.)*	better
exacto *(adj.)*	correct, exact
retrato *(m.n.)*	portrait
error *(m.n.)*	error
impresión *(f.n.)*	impression
actitud *(f.n.)*	attitude
matrimonio *(m.n.)*	marriage, married couple
cuadro *(m.n.)*	square, picture
instinto *(m.n.)*	instinct
bastante *(adj.)*	sufficient
sostener	to sustain
sostengo	sostenemos
sostienes	sostenéis
sostiene	sostienen
acuerdo *(m.n.)*	agreement, sense(s)
espacio *(m.n.)*	space
patria *(f.n.)*	native land
¡oh! (interj.)	oh!
solución *(f.n.)*	solution
fecha *(f.n.)*	date
ochenta *(num.)*	eighty

amar	to love
sitio *(m.n.)*	place
llenar	to fill
fe *(f.n.)*	faith
vital *(adj.)*	living, vital
presente *(adj.)*	present
disposición *(f.n.)*	disposition
fortuna *(f.n.)*	fortune
expresión *(f.n.)*	expression
pleno *(adj.)*	full
habitación *(f.n.)*	room, dwelling
juicio *(m.n.)*	judgment, reason, opinion
medida *(f.n.)*	size, measure(ment)
establecer	to establish

establezco		establecemos	
estableces		establecéis	
establece		establecen	

salvar	to save, reach
particular *(adj.)*	private, particular
jamás *(adv.)*	never
convencer	to convince

convenzo		convencemos	
convences		convencéis	
convence		convencen	

guardia *(f.n.) (m.n.)*	guard, police(woman), policeman
procurar	to try, get, manage (to)

clásico *(adj.)*	classical
desaparecer	to disappear
desaparezco	desaparecemos
desapareces	desaparecéis
desaparece	desaparecen
ilusión *(f.n.)*	illusion
peligro *(m.n.)*	danger
carne *(f.n.)*	meat, flesh
verso *(m.n.)*	verse, line (of poetry)
visión *(f.n.)*	vision
convento *(m.n.)*	monastery; (de monjas, nunnery)
dulce *(adj.)*	sweet, gentle
exigir	to demand, need
exijo	exigimos
exiges	exigís
exige	exigen
base *(f.n.)*	base, basis
determinado *(adj.)*	fixed, certain
arma *(f.n.)*	arm, weapon
raza *(f.n.)*	race
compañía *(f.n.)*	company
tía *(f.n.)*	aunt
dedicar	to dedicate
suma *(f.n.)*	sum(mary)
detalle *(m.n.)*	detail, gesture, bill
octavo *(adj.)*	eighth

central *(adj.)*	central
café *(m.n.)*	coffee, café
diferencia *(f.n.)*	difference
tradición *(f.n.)*	tradition
acerca *(adv.)*	approximately
republicano *(adj.)*	republican
construcción *(f.n.)*	construction
prestar	to lend
entero *(adj.)*	whole, entire
citar	to cite, make an appointment
ideal *(m.n.)*	ideal
academia *(f.n.)*	academy
límite *(m.n.)*	limit, extreme
planta *(f.n.)*	plan(t), storey
pobre *(adj.)*	poor
absoluto *(adj.)*	absolute
eterno *(adj.)*	eternal
barco *(m.n.)*	boat, ship
mayoría *(f.n.)*	majority
construir	to construct

construyo	construimos
construyes	construís
construye	construyen

breve *(adj.)*	short, brief
coger	to take hold of, pick (up), catch (up) (with)
cojo	cogemos
coges	cogéis
coge	cogen
creación *(f.n.)*	creation
declarar	to declare
verde *(adj.)*	green
caber	to go (in), fit, happen
quepo	cobemos
cabes	cabéis
cabe	caben
alegre *(adj.)*	happy, merry
delante *(adv.)*	in front, ahead
jurar	to swear
geográfico *(adj.)*	geographic(al)
despertar	to wake (up), awaken
despierto	despertamos
despiertas	despertáis
despierta	despiertan
extranjero *(adj.)*	foreign
magnífico *(adj.)*	magnificent
plan *(m.n.)*	plan, basis
físico *(adj.)*	physical
juego *(m.n.)*	game, set, play
práctico *(adj.)*	practical
desarrollo *(m.n.)*	development
junta *(f.n.)*	meeting, commitee, junta
reunir	to gather, assemble, get together

distancia *(f.n.)*	distance
artístico *(adj.)*	artistic
hoja *(f.n.)*	leaf, sheet
famoso *(adj.)*	famous
junto *(adv.)*	together
dificultad *(f.n.)*	difficulty
pared *(f.n.)*	wall
labio *(m.n.)*	lip
escena *(f.n.)*	scene, stage
conversación *(f.n.)*	conversation
santa *(f.n.)*	(female) saint
corte *(f.n.)*	court (Cortes, Parliament)
gozar	to enjoy
belleza *(f.n.)*	beauty
proceder	to proceed
presidente (m.n., f.n.)	president
capitán *(m.n.)*	captain
ancho *(adj.)*	broad, wide
obligar	to oblige
dato *(m.n.)*	fact

solamente *(adv.)*	only
leyenda *(f.n.)*	legend
lengua *(f.n.)*	tongue, language
imaginar	to imagine
matemática *(f.n.)*	mathematics
cortar	to cut
muchacho *(m.n.)*	boy, lad
propiedad *(f.n.)*	property, accuracy
gesto *(m.n.)*	face, gesture
montaña *(f.n.)*	mountain
hogar *(m.n.)*	fireplace, home
vuestro *(adj.)*	your
avanzar	to advance, promote
entregar	to deliver, hand (over), (in)
materia *(f.n.)*	material, matter
extender	to extend
extiendo	extendemos
extiendes	extendéis
extiende	extienden
nuevo *(m.n.)*	(the) new
plata *(f.n.)*	money, silver
adelante *(adv.)*	forward, onward, ahead
aumentar	to increase

Unit 46

enfermo *(adj.)*	ill
puerto *(m.n.)*	port
espiritual *(adj.)*	spiritual
lectura *(f.n.)*	reading
contener	to contain
contengo	contenemos
contienes	contenéis
contiene	contienen
lente (m.n., f.n.)	lens
cualquiera *(pron.)*	whatever, whoever
moral *(adj.)*	moral
cabo *(m.n.)*	end, cape
pertenecer	to belong
pertenezco	pertenecemos
perteneces	pertenecéis
pertenece	pertenecen
tren *(m.n.)*	train
defensa *(f.n.)*	defence
profesor *(m.n.)*	teacher, professor (m.)
profesora *(f.n.)*	teacher, professor (f.)
enfermedad *(f.n.)*	illness
precioso *(f.n.)*	precious
rostro *(m.n.)*	face
comunicar	to communicate
dado *(adj.)*	given
civilización *(f.n.)*	civilization
fino *(adj.)*	fine refined

Unit 47

mucho *(pron.)*	a lot
surgir	to spring (up), arise
surjo	surgimos
surges	surgís
surge	surgen
abandonar	to abandon
estructura *(f.n.)*	structure
verano *(m.n.)*	summer
maravilloso *(adj.)*	wonderful
evitar	to avoid
tranquilo *(adj.)*	calm
curso *(m.n.)*	course
precio *(m.n.)*	price
culpa *(f.n.)*	blame, guilt, sin
sabio *(m.n.)*	scholar, wise man
europeo *(adj.)*	European
loco *(adj.)*	mad
naturalmente *(adv.)*	naturally
unido *(adj.)*	united
estilo *(m.n.)*	style
pena *(f.n.)*	grief, trouble, punishment
ángel *(m.n.)*	angel, charm
príncipe *(m.n.)*	prince

Unit 48

espejo *(m.n.)*	mirror
prensa *(f.n.)*	press
edificio *(m.n.)*	building
oficial *(adj.)*	official
revista *(f.n.)*	review
frecuencia *(f.n.)*	frequency
temer	to fear
grito *(m.n.)*	shout, cry
divino *(adj.)*	divine
capaz *(adj.)*	capable, capacious
romper	to break
curiosidad *(f.n.)*	curiosity
eje *(m.n.)*	axis, axle
íntimo *(adj.)*	intimate
sonar	to play, sound
sueno	sonamos
suuenas	sonáis
suena	suenan
negocio *(m.n.)*	affair, business, deal
tirar	to throw (away), shoot, pull
distinguir	to distinguish
distingo	distinguimos
distingues	distinguís
distingue	distinguen
substancia *(f.n.)*	substance
conferencia *(f.n.)*	conference

chico *(m.n.)*	boy, lad
diferente *(adj.)*	different
pecho *(m.n.)*	chest, breast
luminoso *(adj.)*	bright, shining
respeto *(m.n.)*	respect
amplio *(adj.)*	ample, spacious
superficie *(f.n.)*	surface
engañar	to deceive, mislead
modelo *(m.n.)*	model
hambre *(f.n.)*	hunger
inteligencia *(f.n.)*	intelligence
muerto *(adj.)*	dead
personal *(adj.)*	personal
ayudar	to help
corto *(adj.)*	short
pregunta *(f.n.)*	question
terrible *(adj.)*	terrible
crítica *(f.n.)*	criticism
ignorar	not to know
directo *(adj.)*	direct

preferir	to prefer
prefiero	preferimos
prefieres	preferís
prefiere	prefieren
doce *(m.n.)*	twelve
abierto *(adj.)*	open
beber	to drink
fantasía *(f.n.)*	fantasy
inmenso *(adj.)*	immense
seguida *(f.n.)*	proper way (en seguida, right away)
tabla *(f.n.)*	board, shelf, table
visita *(f.n.)*	visit
atreverse	to dare
impedir	to hinder
impido	impedimos
impides	impedís
impide	impiden
matemático *(adj.)*	mathematical
novio *(f.n.)*	fiancé, sweetheart, bridegroom
suceso *(m.n.)*	incident, event
amo *(m.n.)*	master, owner
suave *(adj.)*	gentle, mild
piel *(f.n.)*	skin
laboratorio *(m.n.)*	laboratory
detrás *(adv.)*	behind
especialmente *(adv.)*	especially

rojo *(adj.)*	red
alemán *(adj.)*	German
deber *(m.n.)*	duty, debt
esencial *(adj.)*	essential
perfectamente *(adv.)*	perfectly
caballo *(m.n.)*	horse
enviar	to send
envío	enviamos
envías	enviáis
envía	envían
sensación *(f.n.)*	sensation
arrancar	to spring (up, out), tear (away, off), snatch
pan *(m.n.)*	bread, loaf
puesto *(m.n.)*	position, post
bonito *(adj.)*	pretty
carrera *(f.n.)*	race, run, rush, route
continuación *(f.n.)*	continuation
mitad *(f.n.)*	half, middle
conforme *(adj.)*	agreed, alike, consistent
penetrar	to penetrate
lanzar	to throw (out, down, up)
demasiado *(adv.)*	too (much)
golpe *(m.n.)*	blow, coup

pelo *(m.n.)*	hair
individuo *(m.n.)*	individual
villa *(f.n.)*	villa, small town
hondo *(adj.)*	deep, low
dominar	to dominate
exposición *(f.n.)*	exhibition
vestido *(adj.)*	dressed
andaluz *(adj.)*	Andalusian
personalidad *(f.n.)*	personality
pieza *(f.n.)*	piece, room, play
pasado *(m.n.)*	past
unidad *(f.n.)*	unit(y)
remedio *(m.n.)*	remedy
inglés *(m.n.)*	Englishman
seco *(adj.)*	dry, brusque
conde *(m.n.)*	count
dudar	to doubt
terreno *(m.n.)*	(piece of) land, ground
ánimos *(m.n.)*	mind, spirit, courage
vuelta *(f.n.)*	turn, bend

representación *(f.n.)*	representation, performance
novelista (m.n., f.n.)	novelist
cristal *(m.n.)*	glass, crystal
serio *(adj.)*	serious
columna *(f.n.)*	column
filosofía *(f.n.)*	philosophy
debajo *(adv.)*	under(neath)
pluma *(f.n.)*	pen, feather
limitar	to limit
acordar(se)	to agree, decide, recall
acuerdo	acordamos
acuerdas	acordáis
acuerda	acuerdan
resto *(m.n.)*	rest, (restos, remains)
completamente *(adv.)*	completely
domingo *(m.n.)*	Sunday
fórmula *(f.n.)*	formula
imposible *(adj.)*	impossible
escapar	to escape
seguramente *(adv.)*	surely
porvenir *(m.n.)*	future
medicina *(f.n.)*	medicine
mío *(pron.)*	mine

traje *(m.n.)*	dress, suit
producto *(m.n.)*	product
curioso *(adj.)*	curious
económico *(adj.)*	economic(al)
noble *(adj.)*	noble
ibérico *(adj.)*	Iberian
joven *(adj.)*	young
mañana *(adv.)*	tomorrow
junto *(adj.)*	together, next to
fuente *(f.n.)*	spring, fount(ain)
marquesa *(f.n.)*	marchioness
presencia *(f.n.)*	presence
viajero *(m.n.)*	traveller
raíz *(f.n.)*	root
socialista (m.n., f.n.)	socialist
criatura *(f.n.)*	creature
extremo *(m.n.)*	extreme
universal *(adj.)*	universal
cultural *(adj.)*	cultural
éxito *(m.n.)*	success, result

soldado *(m.n.)*	soldier
examinar	to examine
francés *(m.n.)*	Frenchman
cuanto *(pron.)*	as much as
generación *(f.n.)*	generation
poesía *(f.n.)*	poetry, poem
unir	to unite
anoche *(adv.)*	last night
metal *(m.n.)*	metal
religión *(f.n.)*	religion
sorprender	to surprise
criterio *(m.n.)*	criterion
interpretación *(f.n.)*	interpretation
definición *(f.n.)*	definition
separar	to separate
viejo *(adj.)*	old
extensión *(f.n.)*	extention
industria *(f.n.)*	industry
cantidad *(f.n.)*	quantity
mamá *(f.n.)*	mummy, mom

parar	to stop, parry
comercio *(m.n.)*	commerce
riqueza *(f.n.)*	wealth
cama *(f.n.)*	bed
gris *(adj.)*	grey
tender	to spread (out), stretch (out), tend
tiendo	tendemos
tiendes	tendéis
tiende	tienden
humanidad *(f.n.)*	humanity
comedia *(f.n.)*	comedy
lejano *(adj.)*	distant
tendencia *(f.n.)*	tendency
viento *(m.n.)*	wind
resolver	to (re)solve
resuelvo	resolvemos
resuelves	resolvéis
resuelve	resuelven
usar	to use
categoría *(f.n.)*	category
música *(f.n.)*	music
desarrollar	to develop, unfold
alguien *(pron.)*	someone, anybody
sencillo *(adj.)*	simple
triunfo *(m.n.)*	triumph
apuntar	to point (at), (to), (out), note (down), show

expresar	to express
material *(m.n.)*	material(s), equipment
señorito *(m.n.)*	young gentleman
brillante *(adj.)*	brilliant
fenómeno *(m.n.)*	phenomenon
habitante (m.n., f.n.)	inhabitant
¿adonde? *(adv.)*	where?
cerrado *(adj.)*	closed, thick, overcast
manifestar	to show, reveal
manifiesto	manifestamos
manifiestas	manifestáis
manifiesta	manifiestan
semejante *(adj.)*	similar
genio *(m.n.)*	genius, disposition
perro *(m.n.)*	dog
trasladar	to move, transfer, translate
aquélla *(pron.)*	that, former (f.)
conducir	to take, carry, drive, guide
conduzco	conducimos
conduces	conducís
conduce	conducen
cristiano *(adj.)*	Christian
facultad *(f.n.)*	faculty
cargo *(m.n.)*	charge, load, duty
mérito *(m.n.)*	merit
acostar	to lay down, lie down
acuesto	acostamos
acuestas	acostáis
acuesta	acuestan

felicidad *(f.n.)*	happiness
ángulo *(m.n.)*	angle, corner
muro *(m.n.)*	wall
actor *(m.n.)*	actor
comisión *(f.n.)*	commission
oficio *(m.n.)*	job, trade, office
aprovechar	to profit (by) (from), (be of) use
derecha *(f.n.)*	right (hand) (side)
doctrina *(f.n.)*	doctrine
territorio *(m.n.)*	territory
contrario *(m.n.)*	contrary
análogo *(adj.)*	analogous
fundamental *(adj.)*	fundamental
mentira *(f.n.)*	lie
asomar	to show
despedir	to say goodbye, see (off), (out), dismiss

despido	despedimos
despides	despedís
despide	despiden

ensayo *(m.n.)*	essay
ilustre *(adj.)*	illustrious
rosa *(f.n.)*	rose
mal *(m.n.)*	evil, misfortune, illness

tío *(m.n.)*	uncle
contemporáneo *(adj.)*	contemporary
fundar	to found
permanecer	to remain
permanezco	permanecemos
permaneces	permanecéis
permanece	permanecen
organizar	to organize
admirable *(adj.)*	admirable
causar	to cause
encerrar	to shut (up), (in), lock (up), (in), include
encierro	encerramos
encierras	encerráis
encierra	encierran
aplicación *(f.n.)*	application
bastante *(adv.)*	sufficiently
frontera *(f.n.)*	frontier
descubrimiento *(m.n.)*	discovery
boda *(f.n.)*	wedding, marriage
procedimiento *(m.n.)*	process, procedure
anunciar	to announce
romano *(adj.)*	Roman
ocultar	to hide
misterio *(m.n.)*	mystery
célula *(f.n.)*	cell
iniciar	to begin, initiate

circunstancia *(f.n.)*	circumstance
animal *(m.n.)*	animal
esperanza *(f.n.)*	hope
constante *(adj.)*	constant
frío *(adj.)*	cold
reciente *(adj.)*	recent
amistad *(f.n.)*	friendship
interior *(adj.)*	interior, inner
sala *(f.n.)*	room, hall
mas *(conj.)*	but
incluso *(adj.)*	enclosed, inclusive
museo *(m.n.)*	museum
aventura *(f.n.)*	adventure
griego *(adj.)*	Greek
justo *(adj.)*	just, right, exact
cubrir	to cover
baile *(m.n.)*	dance, ball, ballet
satisfacción *(f.n.)*	satisfaction
monte *(m.n.)*	mountain
lección *(f.n.)*	lesson, class

probar	to prove, try, test
pruebo	probamos
pruebas	probáis
prueba	prueban
romántico *(adj.)*	romantic
vera *(f.n.)*	edge, bank, border
sur *(m.n.)*	south
discutir	to discuss, argue (about), (against)
agradecer	to be grateful, thank
agradezco	agradecemos
agradeces	agradecéis
agradece	agradecen
papá *(m.n.)*	daddy, pop
suyo *(pron.)*	his, hers, its, yours, theirs
elegante *(adj.)*	elegant
isla *(f.n.)*	island
división *(f.n.)*	division
talento *(m.n.)*	talent
inquietud *(f.n.)*	worry, restlessness
comida *(f.n.)*	food, meal
intención *(f.n.)*	intention
setenta *(num.)*	seventy
torre *(f.n.)*	tower
bondad *(f.n.)*	goodness
conjunto *(m.n.)*	whole, ensemble
pronunciar	to pronounce

Unit 62

resistir	to resist
atravesar	to cross (over), lay across
atravieso	atravesamos
atraviesas	atravesáis
atraviesa	atraviesan
arriba *(adv.)*	above, overhead, up
paisaje *(m.n.)*	landscape
comienzo *(m.n.)*	beginning, inception
liberal *(adj.)*	liberal
dieciseis *(num.)*	sixteen
rayo *(m.n.)*	ray, lightning
marcha *(f.n.)*	march, walk, speed
apreciar	to appreciate
padecer	to suffer
padezco	padecemos
padeces	padecéis
padece	padecen
proceso *(m.n.)*	process(ing), trial
debido *(adj.)*	due, proper
broma *(f.n.)*	fun, joke
video *(m.n.)*	video (recorder)
tropa *(f.n.)*	troop, crowd
tropezar	to trip, run (into), (up against)
virtud *(f.n.)*	virtue
espalda *(f.n.)*	shoulder, back
madera *(f.n.)*	wood
gritar	to shout
falso *(adj.)*	false

ejemplar *(m.n.)*	example, copy, specimen
camarada (m.n., f.n.)	comrade, pal
contacto *(m.n.)*	contact
digno *(adj.)*	worthy
original *(adj.)*	original
ingenio *(m.n.)*	wit, ingenuity
borde *(m.n.)*	edge, border, side
confesar	to confess
confieso	confesamos
confiesas	confesáis
confiesa	confiesan
elevar	to raise, promote
cálculo *(m.n.)*	calculation
sonréir	to smile
sonrío	sonreímos
sonríes	sonréis
sonríe	sonríen
blanco *(m.n.)*	white(ness)
molestar	to annoy, disturb
altura *(f.n.)*	height, depth, latitude
crítico *(m.n.)*	critic
mencionar	to mention
tras *(prep.)*	behind, beyond, after
preocupación *(f.n.)*	preoccupation
duque *(m.n.)*	duke
regla *(f.n.)*	rule(r), regulation

pesar *(m.n.)*	regret, grief
comprobar	to check, prove
compruebo	comprobamos
compruebas	comprobáis
comprueba	comprueban
estrella *(f.n.)*	star
novedad *(f.n.)*	novelty
cruzar	to cross
rápido *(adj.)*	quick
volumen *(m.n.)*	volume
confianza *(f.n.)*	confidence, trust
biblioteca *(f.n.)*	library
componer	to compose
compongo	componemos
compones	componéis
compone	componen
filósofo *(m.n.)*	philosopher
vencer	to beat, win, conquer
venzo	vencemos
vences	vencéis
vence	vencen
remoto *(adj.)*	remote
profesión *(f.n.)*	profession
nada *(f.n.)*	nothingness, void
educar	to educate
dispuesto *(adj.)*	disposed
excelente *(adj.)*	excellent
italiano *(adj.)*	Italian
par *(m.n.)*	couple, pair

aquello *(pron.)*	that, former (m.)
satisfacer	to satisfy
satisfago	satisfacemos
satisfaces	satisfacéis
satisface	satisfacen
escrito *(adj.)*	written
definir	to define
once *(num.)*	eleven
tono *(m.n.)*	tone
cuidar	to care (for), (of), mind
historiador *(m.n.)*	historian
piso *(m.n.)*	floor, storey
arco *(m.n.)*	arc, arch(way)
costar	to cost
cuesto	costamos
cuestas	costáis
cuesta	cuestan
barba *(f.n.)*	beard
cincuenta *(num.)*	fifty
saludar	to greet
proyecto *(m.n.)*	project, plan
enseñanza *(f.n.)*	education, teaching
fruto *(m.n.)*	fruit
limpio *(adj.)*	clean
publicado *(adj.)*	published
entrada *(f.n.)*	entrance, entry

Unit 66

internacional *(adj.)* — international
querido *(adj.)* — dear, darling
energía *(f.n.)* — energy
concedir — to concede
fábrica *(f.n.)* — factory, manufacture
santo *(m.n.)* — saint
pintar — to paint
deducir — to deduce, deduct

deduzco	deducimos
deduces	deducís
deduce	deducen

cariño *(m.n.)* — affection, fondness
sección *(f.n.)* — section
atender — to attend (to), serve, care for

atiendo	atendemos
atiendes	atendéis
atiende	atienden

revolucionario *(adj.)* — revolutionary
cámara *(f.n.)* — chamber, room
oscuro *(adj.)* — dark, obscure
escaso *(adj.)* — scarce, thin, scanty
representante (m.n., f.n.) — representative
volar — to fly

vuelo	volamos
vuelas	voláis
vuela	vuelan

sacrificio *(m.n.)* — sacrifice
inferior *(adj.)* — lower, inferior
producción *(f.n.)* — production

pierna *(f.n.)*	leg
horizonte *(m.n.)*	horizon
remoto *(adj.)*	remote
nube *(f.n.)*	cloud
constitución *(f.n.)*	constitution
lenguaje *(m.n.)*	language
posibilidad *(f.n.)*	possibility
nervio *(m.n.)*	nerve
modesto *(adj.)*	modest
romanticismo *(m.n.)*	Romanticism
alzar	to raise (up), lift (up)
fijo *(adj.)*	fixed
bandera *(f.n.)*	flag, standard
esposa *(f.n.)*	wife
salud *(f.n.)*	health
poderoso *(adj.)*	powerful
imperio *(m.n.)*	empire
enterar	to inform, tell, pay
sindicato *(m.n.)*	trade union, syndicate
bosque *(m.n.)*	wood(land), forest

torno *(m.n.)*	bend, lathe, brake ('en torno a', 'round, about')
edición *(f.n.)*	edition, publishing
pintor (m.n., f.n.)	painter
salón *(m.n.)*	drawing-room, lounge, parlour
preocupar	to preoccupy
institución *(f.n.)*	institution
patio *(m.n.)*	patio, court(yard)
crisis *(f.n.)* (pl. las crisis)	crisis
estudiante (m.n., f.n.)	student
rodear	to surround, enclose, shut in
operación *(f.n.)*	operation
arquitectura *(f.n.)*	architecture
retirar	to move (away, back), withdraw, retire
idioma *(m.n.)*	language
seguridad *(f.n.)*	security
suya *(pron.)*	your(s), his, hers, its, their(s)
inmediatamente *(adv.)*	inmediately
director *(m.n.)* (f.n. directriz)	director, manager
inmediato *(adj.)*	immediate
durar	to last, survive, continue

Unit 69

americano *(adj.)*	American
crecer	to grow
crezco	crecemos
creces	crecéis
crece	crecen
vía *(f.n.)*	road, route, way, system
abuelo *(m.n.)*	grandfather
determinar	to determine, decide
izquierda *(f.n.)*	left(hand)(side)
prisa *(f.n.)*	hurry, haste
mientras *(conj.)*	while, as long as
cansar	to tire, fatigue (cansarse, to get tired)
técnico *(adj.)*	technical
sereno *(adj.)*	serene, peaceful
viuda *(f.n.)*	widow
árabe *(adj.)*	Arab(ic)
comparar	to compare
diario *(m.n.)*	newspaper, diary
misterioso *(adj.)*	mysterious
primitivo *(adj.)*	primitive
dividir	to divide
constar	to be clear, available, known
todos *(pron.)*	all, everything

conducta *(f.n.)*	conduct, management
siquiera *(adv.)*	at least (ni siquiera, not even)
aguardar	to (a)wait, expect
traducir	to translate
traduzco	traducimos
traduces	traducís
traduce	traducen
encanto *(m.n.)*	charm, enchantment
mejor *(m.n.)*	the better, the best
hierro *(m.n.)*	iron
drama *(m.n.)*	drama
admitir	to admit
carretera *(f.n.)*	road, highway
visible *(adj.)*	visible
buque *(m.n.)*	ship
soñar	to dream
diputado *(m.n.)*	representative, deputy
ingeniero *(m.n.)*	engineer
primavera *(f.n.)*	Spring
claridad *(f.n.)*	brightness, clarity
futuro *(adj.)*	future
largo *(m.n.)*	length
declaración *(f.n.)*	declaration

directament *(adv.)*	directly
colonia *(f.n.)*	colony
organismo *(m.n.)*	organization, organism
corriente *(adj.)*	running, normal, current
¡adiós! (interj.)	goodbye!
defecto *(m.n.)*	defect
tristeza *(f.n.)*	sadness
doble *(adj.)*	double
cuarenta *(num.)*	forty
principalmente *(adv.)*	principally
longitud (f.b.)	length, longitude
empresa *(f.n.)*	enterprise
gobernador *(m.n.)*	governor
criado *(m.n.)*	man(servant)
peor *(adj.)*	worse, worst
nombrar	to name, designate
enamorado *(adj.)*	in love
vecino *(m.n.)*	neighbour
documento *(m.n.)*	document
fascismo *(m.n.)*	fascism

dorado *(adj.)*	golden, gilt
extranjero *(m.n.)*	foreign lang(s), alien
apertura *(f.n.)*	opening
inútil *(adj.)*	useless
precisar	to need, specify
cura *(m.n.)* *(f.n.)*	priest, remedy
capa *(f.n.)*	cape, clock, layer
alejar	to move away, remove
ministerio *(m.n.)*	ministry
vestir	to dress, wear
visto	vestimos
vistes	vestís
viste	visten
beso *(m.n.)*	kiss
segundo *(m.n.)*	second
cárcel *(f.n.)*	prison
total *(adj.)*	total
elevado *(adj.)*	high, exalted
atribuir	to atribute
atribuyo	atribuimos
atribuyes	atribuís
atribuye	atribuyen
cesar	to stop, dismiss
facilitar	to facilitate
individual *(adj.)*	individual
definitivo *(adj.)*	definitive, final

imaginación *(f.n.)*	imagination
periodista (m.n., f.n.)	journalist
simpatía *(f.n.)*	liking, affection, charm
contribuir	to contribute
contribuyo	contribuimos
contribuyes	contribuís
contribuye	contribuyen
abajo *(adv.)*	down(wards), (stairs), under(neath)
progreso *(m.n.)*	progress
encender	to light, switch on
enciendo	encendemos
enciendes	encendéis
enciende	encienden
indispensable *(adj.)*	indispensable
menos *(adj.)*	less, fewer, minus
muerto *(m.n.)*	dead person, corpse
descansar	to rest
afirmación *(f.n.)*	affirmation
punto *(f.n.)*	point, end, tip
rojo *(m.n.)*	red (colour)
foco *(m.n.)*	focus, spotlight
oponer	to oppose
opongo	oponemos
opones	oponéis
opone	oponen
primero *(m.n.)*	first (thing)
sospechar	to suspect
únicamente *(adj.)*	solely, uniquely
reacción *(f.n.)*	reaction

desgracia *(f.n.)*	misfortune, accident
actuar	to work, operate, function
actúo	actuamos
actúas	actuáis
actúa	actúan
lástima *(f.n.)*	shame, pity
influir	to influence
influyo	influimos
influyes	influís
influye	influyen
ropa *(f.n.)*	clothes
quejarse	to complain
violento *(adj.)*	violent
adoptar	to adopt
discípulo *(m.n.)*	disciple, pupil
taller *(m.n.)*	workshop, factory
quinto *(adj.)*	fifth
gana *(f.n.)*	desire, wish
misión *(f.n.)*	mission
opuesto *(adj.)*	opposed
amoroso *(adj.)*	loving, affectionate
relativo *(adj.)*	relative
dedo *(m.n.)*	finger, toe
proporcionar	to suppy, provide, lend
colegio *(m.n.)*	school, college
bien *(m.n.)*	advantage, good

kilómetro *(m.n.)*	kilometre
paseo *(m.n.)*	stroll, outing
cifra *(f.n.)*	number
insistir	to insist
creencia *(f.n.)*	belief
obispo *(m.n.)*	bishop
despacho *(m.n.)*	dispatch, office, promptness
prometer	to promise
tardar	to delay, be long, be late
policía *(f.n.)(m.n.)*	police (force), policeman (policía femenino, policewoman)
reina *(f.n.)*	queen
amiga *(f.n.)*	(girl-)friend, lover
reducido *(adj.)*	reduced
hombro *(m.n.)*	shoulder
respuesta *(f.n.)*	answer
ideal *(adj.)*	ideal
soledad *(f.n.)*	solitude, loneliness
clima *(m.n.)*	climate
abuela *(f.n.)*	grandmother, old lady
economía *(f.n.)*	economy, economics

oriental *(adj.)*	eastern, oriental
aparte *(adv.)*	separately, aside
portugués *(adj.)*	Portugese
desnudo *(adj.)*	bare, naked
información *(f.n.)*	information
latín *(adj.)*	Latin
veinticinco *(num.)*	twenty-five
automóvil *(m.n.)*	car
lógico *(adj.)*	logical
mente *(f.n.)*	mind
aldea *(f.n.)*	village
mía *(pron.)*	mine (f.)
conquista *(f.n.)*	conquest
infinito *(adj.)*	infinite
lluvia *(f.n.)*	rain(fall), shower
revolucionar	to rouse to revolt, revolutionize
variedad *(f.n.)*	variety
período *(m.n.)*	period
norma *(f.n.)*	norm
azul *(m.n.)*	blue (colour)

crítico *(adj.)*	critical
por tanto *(conj.)*	so, therefore
temblar	to tremble, shake
virgen *(f.n.)*	virgin
divertir	to amuse, distract
divierto	divertimos
diviertes	divertís
divierte	divierten
juez (m.n., f.n.) (also f. jueza)	judge
inventar	to invent
locura *(f.n.)*	madness
verdaderamente *(adv.)*	really, truly
recién *(adv.)*	just, recently
odio *(m.n.)*	hatred
asustar	to frighten
decisivo *(adj.)*	decisive
reúnion *(f.n.)*	reunion
gasto *(m.n.)*	expense, wear, waste
llave *(f.n.)*	key
adivinar	to foretell, solve
decreto *(m.n.)*	decree
pintura *(f.n.)*	painting
perdido *(adj.)*	lost

chica *(f.n.)*	girl, maid(servant)
nacida *(adj.)*	born
regresar	to return, give back, send back
atacar	to attack
catedral *(f.n.)*	cathedral
formidable *(adj.)*	terrific, redoubtable
aspirar	to breathe in, aspire
ruido *(m.n.)*	noise, commotion, sound
calor *(m.n.)*	heat, warmth
emprender	to underake, attack
seguido *(adj.)*	straight, continuous
caminar	to walk, travel
exclusivamente *(adv.)*	exclusively
tranquilidad *(f.n.)*	calmness
preparado *(adj.)*	prepared
confirmar	to confirm
atrás *(adv.)*	back, behind
final *(m.n.) (f.n.)*	ending, final (sport)
tratado *(m.n.)*	treaty, agreement
presente *(m.n.)*	present

hospital *(m.n.)*	hospital
militar *(m.n.)*	soldier
sexual *(adj.)*	sexual
barrio *(m.n.)*	suburb, district
salida *(f.n.)*	exit, departure
cobre *(m.n.)*	copper
loco *(m.n.)*	lunatic
encargar	to entrust, order, change
recorrer	to travel, go over, cross
unión *(f.n.)*	union
considerado *(adj.)*	considered
respetar	to respect
formación *(f.n.)*	formation
vieja *(f.n.)*	old woman
humilde *(adj.)*	humble
risa *(f.n.)*	laugh(ter)
independiente *(adj.)*	independent
silencioso *(adj.)*	silent
agudo *(adj.)*	sharp, acute
comentar	to comment

máquina *(f.n.)*	machine(ry), engine, camera, car
profesional *(adj.)*	professional
saltar	to jump (over), spring, fly up
afán *(m.n.)*	desire, anxiety, toil
colección *(f.n.)*	collection
hueso *(m.n.)*	bone
matiz *(m.n.)*	shade
heroico *(adj.)*	heroic
quemar	to burn
revelar	to reveal
simpático *(adj.)*	likeable, nice
auténtico *(f.n.)*	genuine
composición *(f.n.)*	composition
hipótesis *(f.n.)* (pl. hipótesis)	hypothesis
paralelo *(adj.)*	parallel
sentado *(adj.)*	seated, sensible
sombrero *(m.n.)*	hat
dictadura *(f.n.)*	dictatorship
ninguno *(pron.)*	nobody, neither
extenso *(adj.)*	extensive

instrucción *(f.n.)*	instruction, knowledge, training
escrito *(m.n.)*	document, writing, brief
integral *(adj.)*	complete, integral
prolongación *(f.n.)*	extensión
miseria *(f.n.)*	poverty, squalor
situado *(adj.)*	situated
sal *(f.n.)*	salt
citado *(adj.)*	aforementioned
apellido *(m.n.)*	family name, surname
contrario *(adj.)*	opposite, contrary
manuscrito *(m.n.)*	manuscript
católico *(adj.)*	Catholic
notable *(adj.)*	notable
lujo *(m.n.)*	luxury
daño *(m.n.)*	damage, injury
práctica *(f.n.)*	practice
serenidad *(f.n.)*	serenity
vino *(m.n.)*	wine
rechazar	to throw back, repel, push away
átome *(m.n.)*	atom

formado *(adj.)*	formed
mercado *(m.n.)*	market
comentario *(m.n.)*	commentary
trágico *(adj.)*	tragic
cultivar	to grow, cultivate
besar	to kiss
tragedia *(f.n.)*	tragedy
mueble *(m.n.)*	piece of furniture (muebles, furniture)
correspondiente *(adj.)*	corresponding
rogar	to beg (for), plead
ruego	rogamos
ruegas	rogáis
ruega	ruegan
ventaja *(f.n.)*	advantage
aplicar	to apply, impose, assign
confundir	to confuse, confound, lose
descender	to drop, lower, take down, descend
desciendo	descendemos
desciendes	descendéis
desciende	descienden
hallazgo *(m.n.)*	find(ing), discovery
cualidad *(f.n.)*	quality
molino *(m.n.)*	mill
sierra *(f.n.)*	mountain-range, saw
ajeno *(adj.)*	outside, foreign, belonging to someone else
cristiano *(adj.)*	Christian

mentir	to lie
miento	mentimos
mientes	mentís
miente	mienten
poético *(adj.)*	poetic
utilizar	to use
concesión *(f.n.)*	concession
instituto *(m.n.)*	institute, school
cueva *(f.n.)*	cave
enamorar	to win love, inspire love (enamorarse, to fall in love)
consentir	to allow, admit, agree
consiento	consentimos
consientes	consentís
consiente	consienten
suficiente *(adj.)*	sufficient
desconocido *(adj.)*	unknown
víctima *(f.n.)*	victim
decidido *(adj.)*	resolute, determined
junio *(f.n.)*	June
local *(adj.)*	local
equivocar	to mistake (equivocarse, to be wrong)
disminuir	to decrease
explicación *(f.n.)*	explanation
disciplina *(f.n.)*	discipline
silla *(f.n.)*	chair
generoso *(adj.)*	generous

pájara *(m.n.)*	bird
interior *(m.n.)*	interior
espectro *(m.n.)*	spectrum, spectre
singular *(adj.)*	singular
calidad *(f.n.)*	quality
fresco *(adj.)*	cool, fresh
poema *(m.n.)*	poem
viajar	to travel
madrileño *(adj.)*	of Madrid
embajador *(m.n.)*	ambassador
infierno *(m.n.)*	hell
rápidamente *(adv.)*	quickly
temperamento *(m.n.)*	temperament
estrecho *(adj.)*	narrow, tight, strict
lágrima *(f.n.)*	tear
nacimiento *(m.n.)*	birth
posterior *(adj.)*	later, back, rear
estético *(adj.)*	aesthetic
banco *(m.n.)*	bank, bench
supremo *(adj.)*	supreme

Unit 85

invierno *(m.n.)*	winter
millar *(m.n.)*	thousand
aconsejar	to advise
estimar	to esteem, estimate
solitario *(adj.)*	lonely, solitary
pasaje *(m.n.)*	passage(way), passing
luchar	to struggle, wrestle
orgullo *(m.n.)*	pride
delicioso *(adj.)*	delicious
amante (m.n., f.n.)	lover
percibir	to perceive, earn
someter	to conquer, submit
firme *(adj.)*	firm, steady
mando *(m.n.)*	command, lead
titulado *(adj.)*	(en)titled
ala *(f.n.)*	wing
glorioso *(adj.)*	glorious
librar	to save, free, deliver
octubre *(m.n.)*	October
indio *(m.n.)*	Indian

angustia *(f.n.)*	anguish, distress
reloj *(m.n.)*	clock, watch
humor *(m.n.)*	humour (U.S. humor)
pobreza *(f.n.)*	poverty
superar	to overcome, excel
municipal *(adj.)*	municipal
vecino *(adj.)*	neighbouring, near(by)
alegrar	to cheer (up) (alegrarse, to be delighted)
tarea *(f.n.)*	job, task
pareja *(f.n.)*	pair, couple
evidente *(adj.)*	evident
sujeto *(m.n.)*	subject
¡bah! (interj.)	bah! Never!
castellano *(adj.)*	Castilian (by extension, Spanish)
rasgo *(m.n.)*	stroke, gesture (pl. features, characteristics)
temor *(m.n.)*	fear
alcalde *(m.n.)*	mayor
cuarto *(adj.)*	fourth
disparar	to shoot
proporción *(f.n.)*	proportion

delicado *(adj.)*	delicate, dainty, choosy
avisar	to inform, tell, warn
batalla *(f.n.)*	battle
substituir	to substitute
substituyo	substituimos
substituyes	substituís
substituye	substituyen
vulgar *(adj.)*	ordinary, vulgar
estancia *(f.n.)*	ranch, farm, stay, dwelling
disco *(m.n.)*	disc(us), disco(theque)
carecer	to lack
carezco	carecemos
careces	carecéis
carece	carecen
evolución *(f.n.)*	evolution
ayuntamiento *(m.n.)*	town or city council, town or city hall
metro *(m.n.)*	metre, underground
sabio *(adj.)*	wise, sensible
variar	to vary
varío	variamos
varías	variáis
varía	varían
actualidad *(f.n.)*	present (time) (pl. actualidades, current events)
ceder	to yield, give away, hand over
cuello *(m.n.)*	neck
impulso *(m.n.)*	impulse
convicción *(f.n.)*	conviction
femenino *(adj.)*	feminine
noventa *(num.)*	ninety

desconocer	disavow
desconozco	desconocemos
desconoces	desconocéis
desconoce	desconocen
franco *(adj.)*	frank, free, clear
crónica *(f.n.)*	chronicle, feature
lento *(adj.)*	slow
sonrisa *(f.n.)*	smile
julio *(m.n.)*	July
plazo *(m.n.)*	period, deadline, instalment
sesenta *(num.)*	sixty
arreglar	to arrange, settle
típico *(adj.)*	typical
alcoba *(f.n.)*	bedroom
mental *(adj.)*	mental
permanente *(adj.)*	permanent
admirar	to admire, surprise
inteligente *(adj.)*	intelligent
miembro *(m.n.)*	member, limb
pasear	to stroll, walk (about)
radio *(f.n.)*	radio
apoyar	to learn, rest, support
conveniente *(adj.)*	convenient

Unit 89

rincón *(m.n.)*	corner
célebre *(adj.)*	famous
arroz *(m.n.)*	rice
griego *(m.n.)*	Greek (language, person)
absurdo *(adj.)*	absurd
¡hola! (interj.)	hullo!
contento *(adj.)*	happy, satisfied
merced *(f.n.)*	favour, reward
paraíso *(m.n.)*	paradise
red *(f.n.)*	net(work)
fácilmente *(adv.)*	easily
deuda *(f.n.)*	debt
bailar	to dance
sexto *(adj.)*	sixth
agradable *(adj.)*	agreeable
ciudadano *(m.n.)*	citizen
mecanismo *(m.n.)*	machinery, mechanism
oriente *(m.n.)*	east, orient
prosa *(f.n.)*	prose
enfermo *(adj.)*	sick

inspirar	to inspire
comunicación *(f.n.)*	communication
excepción *(f.n.)*	exception
firmar	to sign
orientación *(f.n.)*	orientation
colectivo *(adj.)*	collective
definitivamente *(adv.)*	finally
fiel *(adj.)*	faithful
manejo *(m.n.)*	management, confidence, intrigue
programa *(m.n.)*	programme (U.S. program)
acompañado *(adj.)*	accompanied
cadáver *(m.n.)*	corpse
expresivo *(adj.)*	expressive
ladrón *(m.n.)*	thief
órgano *(m.n.)*	organ
medir	to measure
mido	medimos
mides	medís
mide	miden
orilla *(f.n.)*	edge, shore
conclusión *(f.n.)*	conclusion
modo *(f.n.)*	fashion
pintado *(adj.)*	spotted, colourful

nuestro *(pron.)*	ours, of ours
ataque *(m.n.)*	attack
renunciar	to renounce, resign
examen *(m.n.)*	examination
incluir	to include
incluyo	incluimos
incluyes	incluís
incluye	incluyen
siguiera *(conj.)*	even if, even though
agosto *(m.n.)*	August
decisión *(f.n.)*	decision
requerir	to require, send for
requiero	requerimos
requieres	requerís
requiere	requieren
sentimental *(adj.)*	sentimental
ciego *(adj.)*	blind
espléndido *(adj.)*	splendid
peso *(m.n.)*	weight, unit of currency of some Latin American countries
combinación *(f.n.)*	combination, connection, scheme
fraile *(m.n.)*	friar
renacimiento *(m.n.)*	renaissance
terminado *(m.n.)*	ended, finished
aislado *(adj.)*	isolated
descuidar	to neglect, disregard
parlamento *(m.n.)*	parliament

gas *(m.n.)*	gas
resistencia *(f.n.)*	resistance
invisible *(adj.)*	invisible
sensibilidad *(f.n.)*	sensibility
llover	to rain
llueve	rains
vergüenza *(f.n.)*	shame
séptimo *(adj.)*	seventh
útil *(adj.)*	useful
resumen *(m.n.)*	summary
ayuda *(f.n.)*	aid
mediterráneo *(adj.)*	Mediterranean
casino *(m.n.)*	club, casino
combate *(m.n.)*	battle, fight
químico *(adj.)*	chemical
mancha *(f.n.)*	mark, stain
extrañar	to wonder at, deport
continuo *(adj.)*	continuous, continual
cuartel *(m.n.)*	quarter, barracks
establecido *(adj.)*	established
occidental *(adj.)*	western

tontería *(f.n.)*	foolishness
cordial *(adj.)*	friendly
meditar	to meditate, think (over)
gastar	to spend, waste, wear away
débil *(adj.)*	wear
intervención *(f.n.)*	intervention
último *(m.n.)*	(the) last
cruz *(f.n.)*	cross
ansia *(f.n.)*	anxiety, longing
oposición *(f.n.)*	opposition
demonio *(m.n.)*	devil
bolsillo *(m.n.)*	pocker(book), purse
egoísmo *(m.n.)*	egotism
capacidad *(f.n.)*	capacity
distraer	to distract, amuse, relax
distraigo	distraemos
distraes	distraéis
distrae	distraen
tesoro *(m.n.)*	treasure, treasury
pastor *(m.n.)*	shepherd, clergyman
reforma *(f.n.)*	reform(ation), (pl. repairs)
socialista *(adj.)*	socialist
acertar	to manage, get it right

grandeza *(f.n.)*	greatness, size, grandeur
intenso *(adj.)*	intense
oler	to smell (out)
huelo	olemos
hueles	oléis
huele	huelen
político *(m.n.)*	political
amenazar	to threaten
redondo *(adj.)*	round
caja *(f.n.)*	cash(box), cashier's office, box, case
maldito *(adj.)*	damned
polvo *(m.n.)*	dust, powder
ruina *(f.n.)*	ruin
antigüedad *(f.n.)*	age, antique, antiquity
párrafo *(m.n.)*	paragraph
sincero *(adj.)*	sincere
campaña *(f.n.)*	countryside, campaign
asociación *(f.n.)*	association
llegada *(f.n.)*	arrival
diario *(adj.)*	daily
intervenir	to intervene
intervengo	intervenimos
intervienes	intervenís
interviene	intervienen
dueño *(m.n.)*	master, owner, employer
moral *(f.n.)*	morals, morality

justificar	to justify
claro *(adv.)*	clearly
llegado *(adj.)*	arrived
abril *(m.n.)*	April
temporada *(f.n.)*	season, period
chino *(m.n.)*	Chinese
presidencia *(f.n.)*	presidency
recurso *(m.n.)*	recourse, means (pl. resources)
frío *(m.n.)*	cold
dibujo *(m.n.)*	drawing, design
castige *(m.n.)*	punishment
traducción *(f.n.)*	translation
veintiséis *(num.)*	twenty-six
anciono *(m.n.)*	elderly man
baño *(m.n.)*	bath(ing), toilet
enemigo *(adj.)*	enemy
pegar	to hit, strike, stick (on)
voto *(m.n.)*	vote, vow
devolver	to hand back, return
devuelvo	devolvemos
devuelves	devolvéis
devuelve	devuelven
testimonio *(m.n.)*	evidence

dignidad *(f.n.)*	dignity, rank
honrado *(adj.)*	honourable, honest
premio *(m.n.)*	prize
muchedumbre *(f.n.)*	crowd, mob
esposo *(m.n.)*	husband
coronel *(m.n.)*	colonel
dominio *(m.n.)*	domain, dominion
apagar	to put out, switch off
indudable *(adj.)*	undoubted
victoria *(f.n.)*	victory
canción *(f.n.)*	song
prólogo *(m.n.)*	prologue
sorpresa *(f.n.)*	surprise
novia *(f.n.)*	fiancée, bride
empeño *(m.n.)*	determination
expuesto *(adj.)*	exposed, displayed
cocina *(f.n.)*	cookery, cooker, kitchen
integrar	to comprise
violencia *(f.n.)*	violence
curar	to cure, recover

futuro *(m.n.)*	future
concluir	to conclude
concluyo	concluimos
concluyes	concluís
concluye	concluyen
esfera *(f.n.)*	sphere, globe
moro *(m.n.)*	Moor
busca *(f.n.)*	search, (but m.n. bleeping device)
obligación *(f.n.)*	obligation, bond
cenar	to dine
educación *(f.n.)*	education
pálido *(adj.)*	pale
destacar	to emphasize, bring out, detach
rendir	to produce, conquer
rindo	rendimos
rindes	rendís
rinde	rinden
positivo *(adj.)*	positive
elección *(f.n.)*	election
exterior *(adj.)*	external, exterior
cansancio *(m.n.)*	fatigue
decoración *(f.n.)*	decoration
presupuesto *(m.n.)*	budget, estimate
seda *(f.n.)*	silk
escaleral *(f.n.)*	steps, staircase
final *(adj.)*	final

galán *(m.n.)*	handsome man, suitor, male lead
rebelde *(adj.)*	rebellious
prescindir	to omit, dispense with
oportuno *(adj.)*	timely, suitable
constantemente *(adv.)*	constantly
cuerda *(f.n.)*	rope, string, energy
escándalo *(m.n.)*	scandal
pureza *(f.n.)*	purity
transformar	to transform
episodio *(m.n.)*	episode
castillo *(m.n.)*	castle
acontecimiento *(m.n.)*	event
concurrir	to agree, meet, contribute
diecisiete *(m.n.)*	seventeen
elegir	to elect
elijo	elegimos
eliges	elegís
elige	eligen
invitar	to invite
material *(adj.)*	material, physical
probablemente *(adv.)*	probably
tradicional *(adj.)*	traditional
diecinueve *(num.)*	ninteen

amarillo *(adj.)*	yellow
veinticuatro *(num.)*	twenty-four
admiración *(f.n.)*	admiration
multitud *(f.n.)*	multitude
otoño *(m.n.)*	Autumn
grato *(adj.)*	pleasant
jornada *(f.n.)*	hours of work, day's journey
empleado *(m.n.)*	employé
normal *(adj.)*	normal
copiar	to copy
sillón *(m.n.)*	armchair
aludir	to mention
juntar	to join, collect
caracterizar	to characterize
consideración *(f.n.)*	consideration
obligado *(adj.)*	obliged
verde *(m.n.)*	green (colour)
liberalismo *(m.n.)*	liberalism
indefinible *(adj.)*	indefinable
cliente (m.n., f.n.)	client

mayo *(m.n.)*	May
diablo *(m.n.)*	devil
dieciocho *(num.)*	eighteen
tertulia *(f.n.)*	gathering
eficaz *(adj.)*	efficient, effective
democrático *(adj.)*	democratic
introducir	to introduce
introduzco	introducimos
introduces	introducís
introduce	introducen
trato *(m.n.)*	relations(hip), treatment
alumno *(m.n.)*	pupil
culto *(m.n.)*	cult, worship
beneficio *(m.n.)*	benefit, profit, exploitation
marcar	to mark (off, out), score
oficina *(f.n.)*	office, workshop
robar	to rob
empujar	to push
horror *(m.n.)*	horror
sucesión *(f.n.)*	succession
acusar	to show, denounce, reveal
destruir	to destroy
destruyo	destruimos
destruyes	destruís
destruye	destruyen
infantil *(adj.)*	children's

INDEXES

FRENCH KEY WORDS

The basic 2,000-word vocabulary
arranged by frequency in a
hundred units.

With comprehensive French and
English indexes.

Xavier-Yves Escande

The Oleander Press

The Oleander Press
16 Orchard Street
Cambridge
CB1 1JT

www.oleanderpress.com

CONTENTS

Introduction

French Key Words has been designed as an efficient, logical, and practical computer-based word-list for anglophone learners of French in their first year. The basic two thousand 'key' words are so called because by learning these one unlocks the door to several thousand more words: plurals from singulars, feminines from masculines, and parts of the present tense from an infinitive.

The purpose of this technique is to stimulate confidence in the learning of French by teaching the commonest words first, and leaving the less common till later. French Key Words is intended to be used with a conventional grammar and a conventional dictionary, but a massive dictionary has been found in practice to unnerve the beginner, while most available readers introduce too early words or ideas which may be arbitrary or advanced. At this sensitive phase, where interest in learning French can be so easily encouraged or discouraged, it is suggested that the student should be asked to learn words in a hundred units of about twenty 'key' words, thus mastering two thousand such words by the end of the first year. Only then will he or she be ready to absorb arbitrary words of low occurrence. Computer-based methods are by now fully familiar in mathematics and the sciences, but statistical sampling has hitherto been rarely practised in language learning, probably because of the difficulty of establishing a sufficiently large sample to make the frequency list reliable. French Key Words is an ideal revision aid for first-year examinations, because you know you must know all these words.

The Units

Each of the hundred units is self-contained, Unit 1 including the twenty commonest key words, Unit 2 the next commonest and so on. The key word is following by an indication of its part of speech: adj., adjective; adv., adverb; conj., conjunction; f.n., feminine noun; m.n., masculine noun; prep., preposition; pron., pronoun. Verbs are not so shown, because they are represented by the infinitive, which is in every case translated beginning with 'to'.

Masculine nouns and adjectives form their feminine by adding e unless otherwise shown. So masculine vert becomes feminine verte. Singular nouns and adjectives form their plural by adding s unless otherwise shown. So singular vert becomes plural verts, and singular verte becomes plural vertes. Le livre vert in the plural becomes les livres verts and la maison verte becomes les maisons vertes.

Regular verbs are conjugated in the present tense in model form in a separate table. The commonest irregular verbs are conjugated in the present tense (of the active voice, indicative mood), wherever their infinitive occurs in the order of frequency. Though verbs appear only under their infinitive form, their position in the units is judged from the total occurrence of all their parts. Occasionally a phrase connected with a word, usually a verb, has been inserted where the phrase is particularly common or could not be constructed without special knowledge.

The Indexes

The two indexes permit the reader to use French Key Words as a basic dictionary, but once again let it be stressed that the best available dictionary should be purchased if it is intended to continue with French past the elementary stage.

Regular Verbs in the Present Tense

First Conjugation
je parle   I speak
tu parles   you (*s.*) speak
il, elle parle   he, she speaks

Parler, to speak
nous parlons   we speak
vous parlez   you (*pl.*) speak
ils, elles parlent   they speak

Second Conjugation
je finis   I finish
tu finis   you (*s.*) finish
il, elle finit   he, she finishes

Finir, to finish
nous finissons   we finish
vous finissez   you (*pl.*) finish
ils, elles finissent   they finish

Third Conjugation
je reçois   I receive
tu reçois   you (*s.*) receive
il, elle reçoit   he, she receives

Recevoir, to receive
nous recevons   we receive
vous recevez   you (*pl.*)receive
ils, elles recoivent   they receive

Fourth Conjugation
je rends   I give up
tu rends   you (*s.*) give up
il, elle rend   he, she gives up

Rendre, to give up, render
nous rendons   we give up
vous rendez   you (*pl.*) give up
ils, elles rendent   they give up

le (*m.*), la (*f.*), l' before vowel or silent 'h', (*pl.* les) *pron.* — the

un (*m.*), une (*f.*) *pron.* — a, an

de *prep.* — of, from

être — to be, being

    je suis — I am   nous sommes — we are

    tu es — you (*s.*) are   vous êtes — you (*pl.*) are

    il, elle est — he, she is   ils, elles sont — they are

et *conj.* — and

à *prep.* — to, at

il (*pl.* ils) *pron.* — he, it (*m.*), they (*m.*)

elle (*pl.* elles) *pron.* — she, it (*f.*), they (*f.*)

ne *adv.* — not

que *pron.* — that, which, whom

du (*m.*), de la (*f.*) (*pl.* des) *prep., pron.* — of the, from the

avoir — to have

    j'ai — I have   nous avons — we have

    tu as — you (*s.*) have   vous avez — you (*pl.*) have

    il, elle a — he, she has   ils, elles ont — they have

ce (*m.*), cette (*f.*) (*pl.*) ces *adj.* — this, these

qui *pron.*	that, which, who
se, s' before vowel or silent 'h' *pron.*	oneself, himself, herself, itself, themselves
en *prep.*	in, into
dans *prep.*	in, into (inside)
au (*m.*), à la (*f.)* or à l' before vowel or silent 'h' *pron.* (*pl.* aux) *prep., pron.*	to the, at the
ce, c' before vowel or silent 'h' *pron.*	it, that
pas *adv.*	not
son (*m.*), sa (*f.*) (*pl.* ses) *adj.*	one's, his, her, its
pour *prep.*	for
plus *adv.*	more
on *pron.*	one (impersonal)
par *prep.*	by
sur *prep.*	on, upon
mais *adv.*	but
tout (*m.*), toute (*f.*) (pl. tous, toutes) *adj.*	all, every

pouvoir — to be able

  je peux — I can

  tu peux — you (*s.*) can

  il, elle peut — he, she can

  nous pouvons — we can

  vous pouvez — you (*pl.*) can

  ils, elles peuvent — they can

avec *prep.* — with

le (*m.*), la (*f.*), (*pl.* les) *pron.* — him, her, it, them (to replace a noun)

faire — to make, do

  je fais — I make

  tu fais — you (*s.*) make

  il, elle fait — he, she makes

  nous faisons — we make

  vous faites — you (*pl.*) make

  ils, elles font — they make

comme *adv.* — as, like

me, m' before vowel or silent "h" *pron.* — me, to me

dire — to say

  je dis — I say

  tu dis — you (*s.*) say

  il, elle dit — he, she says

  nous disons — we say

  vous dites — you (*pl.*) say

  ils, elles disent — they say

y *adv., pron.* — here, there (used only in compounds: J'y suis, j'y reste! Here I am and here I stay; otherwise see ici, là)

en *adv., pron.* — from there, on that account, of it, of them, some (j'en ai, I have some; je n'en ai pas, I haven't any of them)

bien *adv.* — well

lui (*pl.* eux) *pron.* — him, them

ou *conj.* — or

si *conj.* — if

leur *adj.* — their

où *adv.* — where

mon (*m*), ma (*f.*), (*pl.* mes) *pron.* — my

voir — to see
  je vois — I see
  tu vois — you (*s.*) see
  il, elle voit — he, she sees
  nous voyons — we see
  vous voyez — you (*pl.*) see
  ils, elles voient — they see

sans *prep.* — without

même *adj.* — same

notre *adj.* (*pl.* nos) — our

encore *adv.* — still, yet

grand *adj.* — tall, big, large, great

savoir — to know
  je sais — I know
  tu sais — you know
  il, elle sait — he, she knows
  nous savons — we know
  vous savez — you know
  ils, elles savent — they know

quelque *adj., adv.* — some, any

peu *adv.* — little, few

venir — to come
  je viens — I come
  tu viens — you come
  il, elle vient — he, she comes
  nous venons — we come
  vous venez — you come
  ils, elles viennent — they come

aussi *adv.* — as, so, also, too

donner — to give
  je donne — I give
  tu donnes — you (*s.*) give
  il, elle donne — he, she gives
  nous donnons — we give
  vous donnez — you (*pl.*) give
  ils, elles donnent — they give

très *adv.* — very

devoir — to have to, owe, must
  je dois — I must
  tu dois — you must
  il, elle doit — he, she must
  nous devons — we must
  vous devez — you must
  ils, elles doivent — they must

monsieur *n.m.* (*pl.* messieurs) — Mr, sir, gentleman

falloir, il faut — to be necessary, it is necessary

homme *n.m.* — man, husband

tout *adv.* — quite, entirely

petit *adj.*	small, short
jour *n.m.*	day, daylight
autre *adj.*	other
dont *pron.*	from/by/with + whom, which
rien *pron.*	nothing, anything
vouloir	to want
je veux — I want	nous voulons — we want
tu veux — you (*s.*) want	vous voulez — you (*pl.*) want
il, elle veut — he, she wants	ils, elles veulent — they want
trouver	to find
je trouve — I find	nous trouvons — we find
tu trouves — you (*s.*) find	vous trouvez — you (*pl.*) find
il, elle trouve — he, she finds	ils, elles trouvent — they find
moins *adv.*	less
cela, ça	that (fact, thing) e.g. Cela coûte mille francs. That (thing) costs 1,000 francs.
là *adv.*	there (of a place)
même *adv.*	even
non *adv.*	no, not
croire	to believe, think
je crois — I believe	nous croyons — we believe
tu crois — you (*s.*) believe	vous croyez — you (*pl.*) believe
il, elle croit — he, she believes	ils, elles croient — they believe
quand *conj.*	when
prendre	to take
je prends — I take	nous prenons — we take
tu prends — you (*s.*) take	vous prenez — you (*pl.*) take
il, elle prend — he, she takes	ils, elles prennent — they take
si *adv.*	so, so much
premier (*m.*), première (*f.*)	first
temps *n.m.*	time, weather
toujours *adv.*	always, ever

celui (*m.*), celle (*f.*), (*pl.*)ceux, celles *pron.*	he, she, they, that, those
heure *n.f.*	hour, time
tout *pron.*	all, everything
bon (*m.*), bonne (*f.*) *adj.*	good, fine, nice
aller	to go
je vais — I go	nous allons — we go
tu vas — you (*s.*) go	vous allez — you (*pl.*) go
il, elle va — he, she goes	ils, elles vont — they go
moi *pron.*	I (stressed), me
seul *adj.*	only, alone, single
alors *adv.*	at that time, then
fois *n.f.*	time (quatre fois, four times)
mettre	to place, put
je mets — I put	nous mettons — we put
tu mets — you (*s.*) put	vous mettez — you (*pl.*) put
il, elle met — he, she puts	ils, elles mettent — they put
vie *n.f.*	life
sous *prep.*	below, under
après *prep.*	after
chose *n.f.*	thing
jamais *adv.*	never, ever
parler	to speak
entre *prep.*	between

donc *conj.*	so, therefore
tenir	to hold
je tiens I hold	nous tenons we hold
tu tiens you (*s.*) hold	vous tenez you (*pl.*) hold
il, elle tient he, she holds	ils, elles tiennent they hold
beau (bel before vowel or silent 'h') (*m.*), belle (*f.*), (*pl.* beaux, belles) *adj.*	beautiful, handsome, fine
autre *pron.*	other
jusque (jusqu' before vowel or silent 'h') *prep.*	until, up to
laisser	to let, leave
quel (*m.*), quelle (*f.*) (*pl.* quels, quelles) *adj.*	what, which
trop *adv.*	too, too much, too many
ici *adv.*	here
chez *prep.*	at, with
depuis *prep.*	since, for
rester	to remain
ainsi *adv.*	so, thus, like this
femme *n.f.*	woman, wife
déjà *adv.*	already, before
certain *adj.*	some, sure, certain
passer	to pass, cross

an *n.m.* — year
demander — to ask
moment *n.m.* — moment
assez *adv.* — enough, sufficiently
connaître — to know (be acquainted with)
   je connais — I know
   tu connais — you (*s.*) know
   il, elle connaît — he, she knows
   nous connaissons — we know
   vous connaissez — you (*pl.*) know
   ils, elles connaissent — they know
ni *conj.* — neither, nor
beaucoup *adv.* — much, a great deal
sembler — seem, appear
nouveau (nouvel before vowel or silent 'h') (*m.*), nouvelle (*f.*), (*pl.* nouveaux, nouvelles) — new
monde *n.m.* — world
tel (*m.*), telle (*f.*), (*pl.* telles) *adj.* — such
dernier (*m.*), dernière (*f.*) *adj.* — last, latest
penser — to think
oeil *n.m.* (*pl.* yeux) — eye
chaque *adj.* — each, every
car *conj.* — because, for
paraître — to seem, appear
   je parais — I seem
   tu parais — you (*s.*) seem
   il, elle paraît — he, she seems
   nous paraissons — we seem
   vous paraissez — you (*pl.*) seem
   ils, elles paraissent — they seem

jeune *adj.*	young
devenir	to become (conjugated like venir)
votre (*s.*), (*pl.* vos)	your
fait *n.m.*	act, occurrence
arriver	to arrive, come
point *n.m.*	point, stitch
seulement *adv.*	only, merely
vers *prep.*	towards, about
guerre *n.f.*	war, warfare
comprendre	to understand, include (conjugated like prendre)

enfin *adv.*	at last, in short
peut-être *adv.*	perhaps, possibly
vivre	to live

je vis	I live	nous vivons	we live
tu vis	you (*s.*) live	vous vivez	you (*pl.*) live
il, elle vit	he, she lives	ils, elles vivent	they live

tant *adv.*	so much
idée *n.f.*	idea
chercher	to seek, look for

je cherche	I seek	nous cherchons	we seek
tu cherches	you (*s.*) seek	vous cherchez	you (*pl.*) seek
il, elle cherche	he, she seeks	ils, elles cherchent	they seek

enfant *m. & n.f.*	child, boy, girl
aucun *pron.*	any(one), no(one)
parce que *conj.*	because

lui (*s.*), leur (*pl.*) *pron.*	to him, to them
pendant *prep.*	during, for, through, while
aujourd'hui *adv.*	today
contre *prep.*	against
maintenant *adv.*	now
mot *n.m.*	word
devant *prep.*	before, in front of
travail *n.m.*	work, labour
permettre	to permit (conjugated like mettre)
maison *n.f.*	house
année *n.f.*	year
vieux, vieil (*m.*), vieille (*f.*) *adj.*	old
avant *prep.*	before
revenir	to return (conjugated like venir)
puis *adv.*	then, next, besides
mieux *adv.*	better
aimer	to love

j'aime	I love	nous aimons	we love
tu aimes	you (*s.*) love	vous aimez	you (*pl.*) love
il, elle aime	he, she loves	ils, elles aiment	they love

question *n.f.*	question, query
près *adv.*	near, close to
coup *n.m.*	knock, blow
part *n.f.*	share, part, portion, piece, slice
souvent *adv.*	often
vrai *adj.*	true
force *n.f.*	strength, force
presque, presqu' before vowel or silent 'h' *adv.*	nearly (with negative, hardly)
soir *n.m.*	evening
porter	to carry, bear, bring, wear

je porte	I carry	nous portons	we carry
tu portes	you (*s.*) carry	vous portez	you (*pl.*) carry
il, elle porte	he, she carries	ils, elles portent	they carry

place *n.f.*	place, seat, square
lorsque, lorsqu' before vowel or silent 'h' *adv.*	(at the moment) when, as soon as, while
nom *n.m.*	name
doute *n.m.*	doubt
lieu *n.m.*	place
madame *n.f.*	Mrs, lady
montrer	to show

je montre	I show	nous montrons	we show
tu montres	you (*s.*) show	vous montrez	you (*pl.*) show
il, elle montre	he, she shows	ils, elles montrent	they show

pays *n.m.*	country, land
côté *n.m.*	side
agir	to act, behave

j'agis	I act	nous agissons	we act
tu agis	you (*s.*) act	vous agissez	you (*pl.*) act
il, elle agit	he, she acts	ils, elles agissent	they act

loin *adv.*	far
nuit *n.f.*	night
appeler, s'appeler	to call, to be called
j'appelle — I call	nous appelons — we call
tu appelles — you (*s.*) call	vous appelez — you (*pl.*) call
il, elle appelle — he, she calls	ils, elles appellent — they call
mois *n.m.*	month
sentir	to feel, smell
je sens — I feel	nous sentons — we feel
tu sens — you (*s.*) feel	vous sentez — you (*pl.*) feel
il, elle sent — he, she feels	ils, elles sentent — they feel
ami *n.m.*	friend
cas *n.m.*	case
façon *n.f.*	manner, way
abord *n.m.*, d'abord *adv.*	access, at first
quoi *pron.*	what
attendre	to wait for, await
j'attends — I wait	nous attendons — we wait
tu attends — you (*s.*) wait	vous attendez — you (*pl.*) wait
il, elle attend — he, she waits	ils, elles attendent — they wait
terre *n.f.*	world, earth
recevoir	to receive
je reçois — I receive	nous recevons — we receive
tu reçois — you (*s.*) receive	vous recevez — you (*pl.*) receive
il, elle reçoit — he, she, receives	ils, elles reçoivent — they receive
main *n.f.*	hand
commencer	to begin
je commence — I begin	nous commençons — we begin
tu commences — you (*s.*) begin	vous commencez — you (*pl.*) begin
il, elle commence — he, she begins	ils, elles commencent — they begin
matin *n.m.*	morning
ville *n.f.*	town
suivre	to follow
je suis — I follow	nous suivons — we follow
tu suis — you (*s.*) follow	vous suivez — you (*pl.*) follow
il, elle suit — he, she follows	ils, elles suivent — they follow
tête *n.f.*	head

comment *adv.*
how

entendre
to hear, mean, intend

    j'entends   I hear   nous entendons   we hear
    tu entends   you (*s.*) hear   vous entendez   you (*pl.*) hear
    il, elle entend   he, she hears   ils, elles entendent   they hear

eau *n.f.* (*pl.* eaux)
water

effet *n.m.*
result, effect

regarder
to look, look at, regard, consider, watch

    je regarde   I look   nous regardons   we look
    tu regardes   you (*s.*) look   vous regardez   you (*pl.*) look
    il, elle regarde   he, she looks   ils, elles regardent   they look

partir
to leave, set out, part

    je pars   I leave   nous partons   we leave
    tu pars   you (*s.*) leave   vous partez   you (*pl.*) leave
    il, elle part   he, she leaves   ils, elles partent   they leave

amour *n.m*
love

possible *adj.*
possible

jouer
to play

    je joue   I play   nous jouons   we play
    tu joues   you (*s.*) play   vous jouez   you (*pl.*) play
    il, elle joue   he, she plays   ils, elles jouent   they play

dès *prep.*
as early as, since

esprit *n.m.*
wit, spirit, mind

affaire *n.f.*
business, affair

entrer
to enter

    j'entre   I enter   nous entrons   we enter
    tu entres   you (*s.*) enter   vous entrez   you (*pl.*) enter
    il, elle entre   he, she enters   ils, elles entrent   they enter

suite *n.f.*
suite, continuation

français *adj.*
French

gens *n.m.* (*pl.*)
men, women, people

cause *n.f.*
cause, legal suit, reason

servir
to serve

    je sers   I serve   nous servons   we serve
    tu sers   you (*s.*) serve   vous servez   you (*pl.*) serve
    il, elle sert   he, she serves   ils, elles servent   they serve

long (*m.*), *longue* (*f.*) *adj.*
long

cœur *n.m.*
heart

corps *n.m.* — body

rappeler — to recall
- je rappelle — I recall
- tu rappelles — you (*s.*) recall
- il, elle rappelle — he, she recalls
- nous rappelons — we recall
- vous rappelez — you (*pl.*) recall
- ils, elles rappellent — they recall

dieu *n.m.* — god

longtemps *adv.* — for a long time

besoin *n.m.* — want, need

raison *n.f.* — reason (avoir raison, to be right)

partie *n.f.* — part, party

répondre — to respond, answer
- je réponds — I answer
- tu réponds — you (s.) answer
- il, elle répond — he, she answers
- nous répondons — we answer
- vous répondez — you (*pl.*) answer
- ils, elles répondent — they answer

état *n.m.* — state,

mouvement *n.m.* — movement, move, motion

ci *adv.* — (in compounds, e.g. par-ci) here

perdre — to lose
- je perds — I lose
- tu perds — you (*s.*) lose
- il, elle perd — he, she loses
- nous perdons — we lose
- vous perdez — you (*pl.*) lose
- ils, elles perdent — they lose

voilà *prep.* — there is, there are, here is, here are

Retrouver — to regain, find again, meet, remember
- je retrouve — I find
- tu retrouves — you (*s.*) find
- il, elle retrouve — he, she finds
- nous retrouvons — we find
- vous retrouvez — you (*pl.*) find
- ils, elles retrouvent — they find

porte *n.f.* — gate, door

sortir — to leave, go or get out
- je sors — I go out
- tu sors — you (*s.*) go out
- il, elle sort — he, she goes out
- nous sortons — we go out
- vous sortez — you (*pl.*) go out
- ils, elles sortent — they go out

compte *n.m.* — account

exemple *n.m.* — example

fin *n.f.* — end, purpose

général *adj.* (*pl.* généraux) — general

rendre — to give back, return

   je rends — I give back
   tu rends — you (*s.*) give back
   il, elle rend — he, she gives back
   nous rendons — we give back
   vous rendez — you (*pl.*) give back
   ils, elles rendent — they give back

valeur *n.f.* — value, worth

fond *n.m.* — back (far side), bottom (of pit, etc.)

surtout *adv.* — above all, especially, mostly

simple *adj.* — simple, single, easy

pourquoi *adv.* — why (question or statement)

droit *n.m.* — right, law, fee

oui *adv.* — yes

apporter — bring, provide (conjugated like porter)

père *n.m.* — father

mesure *n.f.* — measure

écrire — to write

   j'écris — I write
   tu écris — you (*s.*) write
   il, elle écrit — he, she writes
   nous écrivons — we write
   vous écrivez — you (*pl.*) write
   ils, elles écrivent — they write

art *n.m.* — art

présenter — to present, introduce, show

   je présente — I present
   tu présentes — you (*s.*) present
   il, elle présente — he, she presents
   nous présentons — we present
   vous présentez — you (*pl.*) present
   ils, elles présentent — they present

chambre *n.f.* — room, bedroom, chamber

vue *n.f.* — sight, view

plein *adj.* — full, filled, many

blanc (*m.*), blanche (*f.*), (*pl.* blancs, blanches) *adj.* — white

fille *n.f.* — girl, daughter

reprendre — to retake, resume, recover, take again (conjugated like prendre) forme *n.f.* — form, shape

mal *adv.* — badly, ill

offrir — to offer

 j'offre — I offer nous offrons — we offer
 tu offres — you (*s.*) offer vous offrez — you (*pl.*) offer
 il, elle offre — he, she offers ils, elles offrent — they offer

livre *n.m.* — book

pourtant *adv.* — however, nevertheless

pied *n.m.* — foot

puisque (puisqu' before any vowel) *conj.* — since, as, because, like

sorte *n.f.* — manner, kind or sort

gros (*m.*), grosse (*f.*) *adj.* — bulk, fat, big

plusieurs *adj. & pl. pron.* — several, many

oublier — to forget

 j'oublie — I forget nous oublions — we forget
 tu oublies — you (*s.*) forget vous oubliez — you (*pl.*) forget
 il, elle oublie — he, she forgets ils, elles oublient — they forget

d'ailleurs *adv. phr.* — besides

lire — to read

 je lis — I read nous lisons — we read
 tu lis — you (*s.*) read vous lisez — you (*pl.*) read
 il, elle lit — he, she reads ils, elles lisent — they read

rue *n.f.* — road, strect

rencontrer — to meet, come across

 je rencontre — I meet nous rencontrons — we meet
 tu rencontres — you (*s.*) meet vous rencontrez — you (*pl.*) meet
 il, elle rencontre — he, she meets ils, elles rencontrent — they meet

parfois *adv.* — occasionally, sometimes

ouvrir — to open

 j'ouvre — I open nous ouvrons — we open
 tu ouvres — you (*s.*) open vous ouvrez — you (*pl.*) open
 il, elle ouvre — he, she opens ils, elles ouvrent — they open

cher (*m.*), chère (*f.*) *adj.* — dear (of price, in affection) reconnaître — to recognise (conjugated like connaître)

œuvre *n.f.* — work, charity

haut *adj.* — high, tall, upper, top

parmi *prep.* — among, amid, within

suffire — to suffice, be enough
   je suffis   I suffice   nous suffisons   we suffice
   tu suffis   you (*s.*) suffice   vous suffisez   you (*pl.*) suffice
   il, elle suffit   he, she suffices   ils, elles suffisent   they suffice

heureux (*m.*), heureuse (*f.*) *adj.* — happy

malgré *prep.* — in spite of, despite

service *n.m.* — service

arrêter — to stop, arrest
   j'arrête   I stop   nous arrêtons   we stop
   tu arrêtes   you (*s.*) stop   vous arrêtez   you (*pl.*) stop
   il, elle arrête,   he, she stops   ils, elles arrêtent   they stop

lequel (*m.*), laquelle (*f.*),   (*pl.* lesquels, lesquelles) *pron.* — who, whom, which

mauvais *adj.* — bad, evil

apprendre — to learn (conjugated like prendre)

maître *n.m.* — master

fort *adv.* — very, strongly, loudly, hard

continuer — to continue
   je continue   I continue   nous continuons   we continue
   tu continues   you (*s.*) continue   vous continuez   you (*pl.*) continue
   il, elle continue he, she continues   ils, elles continuent   they continue

moyen *n.m.* — means, way

table *n.f.*	table
autour *adv.*	round, about (of place)
action *n.f.*	act, action
exister	to exist
j'existe — I exist	nous existons — we exist
tu existes — you (*s.*) exist	vous existez — you (*pl.*) exist
il, elle existe — he, she exists	ils, elles existent — they exist
face *n.f.*	face
fort *adj.*	strong
loi *n.m.*	law
point *adv.*	not at all
famille *n.f.*	family
route *n.f.*	road, way
expliquer	to explain
j'explique — I explain	nous expliquons — we explain
tu expliques — you (*s.*) explain	vous expliquez — you (*pl.*) explain
il, elle explique — he, she explains	ils, elles expliquent — they explain
problème *n.m.*	problem, issue
dessus *adv.*	above, on, over, top
nombre *n.m.*	number
soleil *n.m.*	sun
quitter	to vacate, leave
je quitte — I vacate	nous quittons — we vacate
tu quittes — you (*s.*) vacate	vous quittez — you (*pl.*) vacate
il, elle quitte — he, she vacates	ils, elles quittent — they vacate
âme *n.f.*	soul, feeling
mort *n.f.*	death
chacun *pron.*	each one, every one
sujet *n.m.*	subject, cause

caractère *n.m.*	character, nature
plaisir *n.m.*	pleasure, delight
autant *adv.*	as much (many), so much (many)
manquer	to miss, lack, be short (il me manque cent francs, I am 100 francs short)
je manque I miss	nous manquons we miss
tu manques you (*s.*) miss	vous manquez you (*pl.*) miss
il, elle manque he, she misses	ils, elles manquent they miss
situation *n.f.*	situation, position
nature *n.f.*	nature
fait *adj.*	ripe, developed, done
siècle *n.m.*	century
libre *adj.*	free
ordre *n.m.*	order
tomber	to fall
je tombe I fall	nous tombons we fall
tu tombes you (*s.*) fall	vous tombez you (*pl.*) fall
il, elle tombe he, she falls	ils, elles tombent they fall
propre *adj.*	proper, clean, own
peuple *n.m.*	people, nation
mourir	to die
je meurs I die	nous mourons we die
tu meurs you (*s.*) die	vous mourez you (*pl.*) die
il, elle meurt he, she dies	ils, elles meurent they die
tard *adj.*	late
air *n.m.*	air
entier (*m.*), entière (*f.*) *adj.*	entire
plutôt *adv.*	rather, on the whole, rather
souvenir *n.m.*	memory, memento, reminder
voix *n.f.*	voice

mère *n.f.* mother

second, deuxième *adj.* second

considérer to consider
 je considère I consider   nous considérons we consider
 tu considères you (*s.*) consider   vous considérez you (*pl.*) consider
 il, elle considère he, she considers   ils, elles considèrent they consider

jeu *n.m.* (*pl.* jeux) game

poser to set, place, put
  je pose I put   nous posons we put
  tu poses you (*s.*) put   vous posez you (*pl.*) put
  il, elle pose he, she puts   ils, elles posent they put

ligne *n.f.* line

vraiment *adv.* truly, really

noir *adj.* black

époque *n.f.* epoch, period, era

humain *adj. ou n.m.* human

garder to keep,
  je garde I keep   nous gardons we keep
  tu gardes you (*s.*) keep   vous gardez you (*pl.*) keep
  il, elle garde he, she keeps   ils, elles gardent they keep

ciel *n.m.* (*pl.* cieux) sky, heaven

apparaître to appear (conjugated like paraître)

personne *n.f.* person

assurer to assure, insure, check, ensure
  j'assure I assure   nous assurons we assure
  tu assures you (*s.*) assure   vous assurez you (*pl.*) assure
  il, elle assure he, she assures   ils, elles assurent they assure

ajouter to add
  j'ajoute I add   nous ajoutons we add
  tu ajoutes you (*s.*) add   vous ajoutez you (*pl.*) add
  il, elle ajoute he, she adds   ils, elles ajoutent they add

effort *n.m.* effort, endeavour

tirer to pull, pull off, shoot
  je tire I pull   nous tirons we pull
  tu tires you (*s.*) pull   vous tirez you (*pl.*) pull
  il, elle tire he, she pulls   ils, elles tirent they pull

argent *n.m.* — money, silver

attention *n.f.* — attention (Attention! Watch out!)

empêcher — to prevent, impede, avoid
  j'empêche I prevent — nous empêchons we prevent
  tu empêches, you (*s.*) prevent — vous empêchez you (*pl.*) prevent
  il, elle empêche he, she prevents — ils, elles empêchent they prevent

journée *n.f.* — day, daytime

manière *n.f.* — manner, way

meilleur *adj.* — better

condition *n.f.* — condition (*pl.* terms)

changer — to change, exchange
  je change I change — nous changeons we change
  tu changes you (*s.*) change — vous changez you (*pl.*) change
  il, elle change he, she changes — ils, elles changent they change

bout *n.m.* — end, extremity

obtenir — to obtain, get
  j'obtiens I obtain — nous obtenons we obtain
  tu obtiens you (*s.*) obtain — vous obtenez you (*pl.*) obtain
  il, elle obtient he, she obtains — ils, elles obtiennent they obtain

important *adj.* — important

semaine *n.f.* — week

instant *n.m.* — moment, instant

prix *n.m.* — price, value

monter — to climb, ascend (conjugated like montrer)

sûr *adj.* — sure

difficile *adj.* — difficult

salle *n.f.* — hall, (large) room

songer — to dream, imagine
  je songe I dream — nous songeons we dream
  tu songes you (*s.*) dream — vous songez you (*pl.*) dream
  il, elle songe he, she dreams — ils, elles songent they dream

travailler — to work (intransitive); worry, practice, improve (transitive)

    je travaille — I work
    tu travailles — you (*s.*) work
    il, elle travaille — he, she works
    nous travaillons — we work
    vous travaillez — you (*pl.*) work
    ils, elles travaillent — they work

demi *adj.* — half

paix *n.f* — peace

sens *n.m.* — sense, direction

parole *n.f.* — word, speech

finir — to finish

    je finis — I finish
    tu finis — you (*s.*) finish
    il, elle finit — he, she finishes
    nous finissons — we finish
    vous finissez — you (*pl.*) finish
    ils, elles finissent — they finish

goût *n.m.* — taste, style

intérêt *n.m.* — interest

différent *adj.* — different

mer *n.m.* — sea

remarquer — to observe, remark

    je remarque — I observe
    tu remarques — you (*s.*) observe
    il, elle remarque — he, she observes
    nous remarquons — we observe
    vous remarquez — you (*pl.*) observe
    ils, elles remarquent — they observe

début *n.m.* — outset, beginning, start

pur *adj.* — pure

détail *n.m.* — detail, retail

tourner — to turn, revolve

    je tourne — I turn
    tu tournes — you (*s.*) turn
    il, elle tourne — he, she turns
    nous tournons — we turn
    vous tournez — you (*pl.*) turn
    ils, elles tournent — they turn

pensée *n.f.* — thought

étude *n.f.* — study

air *n.m.* — appearance

jeter — to throw, cast

    je jette — I throw
    tu jettes — you (*s.*) throw
    il, elle jette — he, she throws
    nous jetons — we throw
    vous jetez — you (*pl.*) throw
    ils, elles jettent — they throw

sentiment *n.m* — feeling, opinion

nombreux (*m.*) nombreuse (*f.*) numerous
adj.
toucher to touch
  je touche I touch nous touchons we touch
  tu touches you (*s.*) touch vous touchez you (*pl.*) touch
  il, elle touche he, she touches ils, elles touchent they touch
objet *n.m.* object
ensemble *adv.* together
occuper to occupy, fill
  j'occupe I occupy nous occupons we occupy
  tu occupes you (*s.*) occupy vous occupez you (*pl.*) occupy
  il, elle occupe he, she occupies ils, elles occupent they occupy
minute *n.f.* minute
vérité *n.f.* truth
honneur *n.m.* honour
milieu *n.m.* middle
essayer to try, taste (wine)
  j'essaie I try nous essayons we try
  tu essaies you (*s.*) try vous essayez you (*pl.*) try
  il, elle essaie he, she tries ils, elles essaient they try
chemin *n.m.* way, road
étranger (*m.*), étrangère (*f.*) foreign, strange
adj.
lumière *n.f.* light
auteur *n.m.* author
découvrir to discover, uncover
je découvre I discover nous découvrons we discover
tu découvres you (*s.*) discover vous découvrez you (*pl.*) discover
il, elle découvre he, she discovers ils, elles découvrent they discover
présence *n.f.* presence
franc *n.m.* franc (unit of currency)
fils *n.m.* son, (with names) junior
accepter to accept
  j'accepte I accept nous acceptons we accept
  tu acceptes you (*s.*) accept vous acceptez you (*pl.*) accept
  il, elle accepte he, she accepts ils, elles acceptent they accept

résultat *n.m.* — result

payer — to pay (conjugated like essayer)

valoir — to be worth
  je vaux I am worth
  tu vaux you (*s.*) are worth
  il, elle vaut he, she is worth
  nous valons we are worth
  vous valez you (*pl.*) worth
  ils, elles valent they are worth

impossible *adj.* — impossible

âge *n.m.* — age

roi *n.m.* — king

représenter — to represent, portray (conjugated like présenter)

ancien (*m.*), ancienne (*f.*) *adj.* — ancient, old, former

descendre — to descend, dismount, alight (conjugated like rendre, prendre)

garçon *n.m.* — boy, bachelor, servant

existence *n.f.* — existence

espérer — to hope
  j'espère I hope
  tu espères you (*s.*) hope
  il, elle espère he, she hopes
  nous espérons we hope
  vous espérez you (*pl.*) hope
  ils, elles espèrent they hope

histoire *n.f.* — history

hier *adv.* — yesterday

grâce *n.f.* — grace, charm, thanks

personne *pron.* — anyone, no one, anybody, nobody

apercevoir — to perceive, glimpse
  j'aperçois I perceive
  tu aperçois you (*s.*) perceive
  il, elle aperçoit he, she perceives
  nous apercevons we perceive
  vous apercevez you (*pl.*) perceive
  ils, elles aperçoivent they perceive

mal *n.m.* (*pl.* maux) — harm, evil, ailment

ah! *interj.* — ah! oh!

retenir — to hold back, retain (conjugated like tenir)

posséder — to possess
  je possède — I possess
  tu possèdes — you (*s.*) possess
  il, elle possède — he, she possesses
  nous possédons — we possess
  vous possédez — you (*pl.*) possess
  ils, elles possèdent — they possess

bras *n.m.* — arm

pareil (*m.*), pareille (*f.*) *adj.* — similar, equal

écouter — to listen
  j'écoute — I listen
  tu écoutes — you (*s.*) listen
  il, elle écoute — he, she listens
  nous écoutons — we listen
  vous écoutez — you (*pl.*) listen
  ils, elles écoutent — they listen

lettre *n.f.* — letter

fleur *n.f.* — flower

société *n.f.* — society, club, company

feu *n.m.* — fire, heat

produire — to produce, yield
  je produis — I produce
  tu produis — you (*s.*) produce
  il, elle produit — he, she produces
  nous produisons — we produce
  vous produisez — you (*pl.*) produce
  ils, elles produisent — they produce

hôtel *n.m.* — hotel, mansion (*but* hôtel de ville, Town Hall)

facile *adj.* — easy, simple

région *n.f.* — region, area

élever — to erect, raise
  j'élève — I raise
  tu élèves — you (*s.*) raise
  il, elle élève — he, she raises
  nous élevons — we raise
  vous élevez — you (*pl.*) raise
  ils, elles élèvent — they raise

travers *n.m.* — breadth, failing (de travers, askew)

guère *adv.* — not much

erreur *n.f.* — error, delusion, mistake

journal *n.m.* (*pl.* journaux) — newspaper, journal

courir — to run
  je cours — I run
  tu cours — you (*s.*) run
  il, elle court — he, she runs
  nous courons — we run
  vous courez — you (*pl.*) run
  ils, elles courent — they run

politique *n.f.* — policy, politics

pauvre *adj.* — poor

bord *n.m.*	board, side, edge
saint *n.m.*	saint
juger	to judge, adjudge, try (case)
je juge — I judge	nous jugeons — we judge
tu juges — you (*s.*) judge	vous jugez — you (*pl.*) judge
il, elle juge — he, she judges	ils, elles jugent — they judge
vite *adv.*	quickly
liberté *n.f.*	freedom, liberty
imposer	to impose, enforce
j'impose — I impose	nous imposons — we impose
tu imposes — you (*s.*) impose	vous imposez — you (*pl.*) impose
il, elle impose — he, she imposes	ils, elles imposent — they impose
cours *n.m.*	course, currency, quotation (money)
conduire	to conduct, drive
je conduis — I drive	nous conduisons — we drive
tu conduis — you (*s.*) drive	vous conduisez — you (*pl.*) drive
il, elle conduit — he, she drives	ils, elles conduisent — they drive
cesser	to cease
je cesse — I cease	nous cessons — we cease
tu cesses — you (*s.*) cease	vous cessez — you (*pl.*) cease
il, elle cesse — he, she ceases	ils, elles cessent — they cease
scène *n.f.*	scene, stage
regard *n.m.*	look, gaze, glance
divers *adj.*	different, various
demain *adv.*	tomorrow
souffrir	to suffer, allow, undergo
je souffre — I suffer	nous souffrons — we suffer
tu souffres — you (*s.*) suffer	vous souffrez — you (*pl.*) suffer
il, elle souffre — he, she suffers	ils, elles souffrent — they suffer
rôle *n.m.*	role, roll, list, function
contraire *n.m*	contrary, opposite
dur *adj.*	hard, tough
faute *n.f*	fault, offence, lack, need
refuser	to refuse, fail
je refuse — I refuse	nous refusons — we refuse
tu refuses — you (*s.*) refuse	vous refusez — you (*pl.*) refuse
il, elle refuse — he, she refuses	ils, elles refusent — they refuse
nécessaire *adj.*	necessary

remettre	to replace, send back, postpone (conjugated like mettre)
gouvernement *n.m.*	government
ensuite *adv.*	then, afterwards
rentrer	return, go/come in/home
tandis que *conj.*	while, whereas
principe *n.m*	principle
ignorer	to ignore, not to know
j'ignore I ignore	nous ignorons we ignore
tu ignores you (*s.*) ignore	vous ignorez you (*pl.*) ignore
il, elle ignore he, she ignores	ils, elles ignorent they ignore
curieux (*m.*), curieuse (*f.*) *adj.*	curious, interested
départ *m.n.*	sorting, departure
simplement *adv.*	simply
demeurer	to remain, stay
je demeure I remain	nous demeurons we remain
tu demeures you (*s.*) remain	vous demeurez you (*pl.*) remain
il, elle demeure he, she remains	ils, elles demeurent they remain
grave *adj.*	heavy, severe, grave
haut *adv.*	above, up
observer	to observe, note, watch
j'observe I observe	nous observons we observe
tu observes you (*s.*) observe	vous observez y ou (*pl.*) observe
il, elle observe he, she observes	ils, elles observent they observe
former	to form, shape, train
je forme I form	nous formons we form
tu formes you (*s.*) form	vous formez you (*pl.*) form
il, elle forme he, she forms	ils, elles forment they form
après *adv.*	afterwards
difficulté *n.f.*	difficulty
compter	to count, charge
je compte I count	nous comptons we count
tu comptes you (*s.*) count	vous comptez you (*pl.*) count
il, elle compte he, she counts	ils, elles comptent they count
parfait *adj.*	perfect
imaginer	to imagine, think
j'imagine I imagine	nous imaginons we imagine
tu imagines you (*s.*) imagine	vous imaginez you (*pl.*) imagine
il, elle imagine he, she imagines	ils, elles imaginent they imagine

rouge *adj.*	red
avant *adv.*	before, formerly, first
rapport *n.m.*	report, relation, profit
manger	to eat
je mange I eat	nous mangeons we eat
tu manges you (*s.*) eat	vous mangez you (*pl.*) eat
il, elle mange he, she eats	ils, elles mangent they eat
inutile *adj.*	useless
atteindre	to attain, reach, hit
j'atteins I attain	nous atteignons we attain
tu atteins you (*s.*) attain	vous atteignez you (*pl.*) attain
il, elle atteint he, she attains	ils, elles atteignent they attain
habitude *n.f.*	custom, habit (d'habitude, usually)
appartenir	to belong (conjugated like tenir)
naturel (*m.*), naturelle (*f.*) *adj.*	natural
joie *n.f.*	joy, delight
impression *n.f.*	impression, print, exposure
chef *n.m.*	head, chief, leader
importance *n.f.*	importance
pas *n.m.*	step (faux pas, false step)
décider	to decide
je décide I decide	nous décidons we decide
tu décides you (*s.*) decide	vous décidez you (*pl.*) decide
il, elle décide he, she decides	ils, elles décident they decide
profond *adj.*	deep, profound
champ *n.m.*	field
lever	to lift, raise
je lève I lift	nous levons we lift
tu lèves you (*s.*) lift	vous levez you (*pl.*) lift
il, elle lève he, she lifts	ils, elles lèvent they lift
doux (*m.*), douce (*f.*) *adj.*	sweet, gently, mild

école *n.f.* — school

particulier (*m.*), particulière (*f.*) *adj.* — private, particular, special

eh! *interj.* — hey!

dormir — to sleep
- je dors — I sleep
- tu dors — you (*s.*) sleep
- il, elle dort — he, she sleeps
- nous dormons — we sleep
- vous dormez — you (*pl.*) sleep
- ils, elles dorment — they sleep

voyage *n.m.* — journey, tour

bas (*m.*), basse (*f.*) *adj.* — low

réalité *n.f.* — reality

visage *n.m.* — face

clair *adj.* — clear, bright

présent *n.m.* — present, gift

acte *n.m.* — action, act

préparer — to prepare
- je prépare — I prepare
- tu prépares — you (*s.*) prepare
- il, elle prépare — he, she prepares
- nous préparons — we prepare
- vous préparez — you (*pl.*) prepare
- ils, elles préparent — they prepare

confiance *n.f.* — confidence, trust

somme *n.f.* — sum, amount (*but* le somme, nap, snooze)

répéter — to repeat, rehearse (*but* je répète)
- je répète — I repeat
- tu répètes — you (*s.*) repeat
- il, elle répète — he, she repeats
- nous répétons — we repeat
- vous répétez — you (*pl.*) repeat
- ils, elles répètent — they repeat

couleur *n.f.* — colour

régime *n.m.* — normal operation, form of government, diet

vivant *adj.* — living

expression *n.f.* — expression

robe *n.f.* — dress, skin (of vegetable, etc.)

tendre — to stretch, tend, lead (conjugated like prendre, rendre)

politique *adj.* — political, shrewd

geste *n.m.* — gesture, movement (*but* la geste, exploit)

saisir — to seize
  je saisis I seize — nous saisissons we seize
  tu saisis you (*s.*) seize — vous saisissez you (*pl.*) seize
  il, elle saisit he, she seizes — ils, elles saisissent they seize

reste *n.m.* — remains

frapper — to strike, hit
  je frappe I hit — nous frappons we hit
  tu frappes you (*s.*) hit — vous frappez you (*pl.*) hit
  il, elle frappe he, she hits — ils, elles frappent they hit

selon *prep.* — according to

court *adj.* — short

intéresser — to interest
  j'intéresse I interest — nous intéressons we interest
  tu intéresses you (*s.*) interest — vous intéressez you (*pl.*) interest
  il, elle intéresse he, she interests — ils, elles intéressent they interest

classe *n.f.* — class, lesson, category, classy

moindre *adj.* — lesser (le, la moindre, least)

vent *n.m.* — wind

ministre *n.m.* — minister,

article *n.m.* — article

exprimer — to express
  j'exprime I express — nous exprimons we express
  tu exprimes you (*s.*) express — vous exprimez you (*pl.*) express
  il, elle exprime he, she expresses — ils, elles expriment they express

mur *n.m.* — wall

vif (*m.*), vive (*f.*) *adj.* — alive, living

hiver *n.m.* — winter

groupe *n.m.* — group

bureau *n.m.*	office, writing-desk, board
science *n.f..*	knowledge, science
pousser	to push
je pousse I push	nous poussons we push
tu pousses you (*s.*) push	vous poussez you (*pl.*) push
il, elle pousse he, she pushes	ils, elles poussent they push
commun *adj.*	common
image *n.f.*	image
accord *n.m.*	agreement (d'accord! agreed!)
peur *n.f.*	fear (j'ai peur, I am afraid)
disposition *n.f.*	layout, disposition
projet *n.m.*	project, scheme
douter	to doubt
je doute I doubt	nous doutons we doubt
tu doutes you (*s.*) doubt	vous doutez you (*pl.*) doubt
il, elle doute he, she doubts	ils, elles doutent they doubt
automobile *n.f.*	car (usually abbreviated to auto)
révéler	to reveal, betray (*but* je révèle)
je révèle I reveal	nous révélons we reveal
tu révèles you (*s.*) reveal	vous révélez you (*pl.*) reveal
il, elle révèle he, she reveals	ils, elles révèlent they reveal
bonheur *n.m.*	success, luck, happiness
réponse *n.f.*	answer, reply
qualité *n.f.*	quality, qualification
léger (*m.*), légère (*f.*) *adj*	light, slight, gentle
évidemment *adv.*	evidently
disparaître	to disappear (conjugated like paraître)
envoyer	to send
j'envoie I send	nous envoyons we send
tu envoies you (*s.*) send	vous envoyez you (*pl.*) send
il, elle envoie he, she sends	ils, elles envoient they send
parti *n.m.*	party, match

oiseau *n.m.* (*pl.* oiseaux)	bird
rire	to laugh
je ris I laugh	nous rions we laugh
tu ris you (*s.*) laugh	vous riez you (*pl.*) laugh
il, elle rit he, she laughs	ils, elles rient they laugh
espèce *n.f.*	kind, sort
succès *n.m.*	success, result
examiner	to examine, scrutinise
j'examine I examine	nous examinons we examine
tu examines you (*s.*) examine	vous examinez you (*pl.*) examine
il, elle examine he, she examines	ils, elles examinent they examine
période *n.f.*	period
annoncer	to announce
j'annonce I announce	nous annonçons we announce
tu annonces you (*s.*) announce	vous annoncez you (*pl.*) announce
il, elle annonce he, she announces	ils, elles annoncent they announce
devoir	to have to, owe
je dois I have to	nous devons we have to
tu dois you (*s.*) have to	vous devez you (*pl.*) have to
il, elle doit he, she has to	ils, elles doivent they have to
signe *n.m.*	sign, symbol
constituer	to form, constitute
je constitue I form	nous constituons we form
tu constitues you (*s.*) form	vous constituez you (*pl.*) form
il, elle constitue he, she forms	ils, elles constituent they form
silence *n.m.*	silence
public (*m.*), publique (*f.*) *adj.*	public
établir	to establish, draw up
j'établis I establish	nous établissons we establish
tu établis you (*s.*) establish	vous établissez you (*pl.*) establish
il, elle établit he, she establishes	ils, elles établissant they establish
histoire *n.f.*	story
figure *n.f.*	figure, face
domaine *n.m.*	domain, field
véritable *adj.*	real, true
bois *n.m.*	wood, forest
chien (*m.*), chienne (*f.*) *n.*	dog
amener	to bring (about), convey (*but*
j'amène I bring	j'amène, I bring)
tu amènes you (*s.*) bring	nous amenons we bring
il, elle amène he, she brings	vous amenez you (*pl.*) bring
	ils, elles amènent they bring

naître

    je nais   I am born

    tu nais   you (*s.*) are born

    il, elle naît   he, she is born

frère *n.m.*

constater

artiste *m. &n.f..*

puissance *n.f.*

admettre

large *adj.*

pouvoir *n.m.*

armée *n.f.*

déclarer

  je déclare   I declare

  tu déclares   you (*s.*) declare

  il, elle déclare   he, she declares

conserver

  je conserve I conserve

  tu conserves you (*s.*) conserve

  il, elle conserve he, she...

soin *n.m.*

échapper

    j'échappe   I escape

    tu échappes   you (*s.*) escape

    il, elle échappe   he, she escapes

marcher

    je marche   I walk

    tu marches   you (*s.*) walk

    il, elle marche   he, she walks

supérieur *adj.*

usine *n.f.*

occasion *n.f.*

dame *n.f.*

traiter

    je traite   I treat

    tu traites   you (*s.*) treat

    il, elle traite   he, she treats

étonner

    j'étonne   I stun

    tu étonnes   you (*s.*) stun

    il, elle étonne   he, she stuns

to be born

    nous naissons   we are born

    vous naissez   you (*pl.*) are born

    ils, elles naissent   they are born

brother

to notice, observe

artist, performer

power, strength

to admit, allow (con. like mettre)

broad, wide, ample

power, force

army

to declare, announce

    nous déclarons   we declare

    vous déclarez   you (*pl.*) declare

    ils, elles déclarent   they declare

to preserve, retain, conserve, keep

    nous conservons   we conserve

    vous conservez you (*pl.*) conserve

    ils, elles conservent   they...

care, attention

to escape

    nous échappons   we escape

    vous échappez you (*pl.*) escape

    ils, elles échappent they escape

to go, walk

    nous marchons   we walk

    vous marchez   you (*pl.*) walk

    ils, elles marchent   they walk

upper, superior

works, factory

occasion, opportunity

lady

to treat

    nous traitons   we treat

    vous traitez   you (*pl.*) treat

    ils, elles traitent   they treat

to stun, astonish, surprise

    nous étonnons   we stun

    vous étonnez   you (*pl.*) stun

    ils, elles étonnent   they stun

distinguer — to distinguish, characterise
  je distingue — I distinguish
  tu distingues — you (*s.*) dist...
  il, elle distingue — he, she dist...
  nous distinguons — we distinguish
  vous distinguez — you (*pl.*) dist...
  ils, elles distinguent — they dist...

poursuivre — to pursue (conjugated like suivre)

musique *n.f.* — music

église *n.f.* — church

mener — to lead, drive, steer (*but* je mène)
  je mène — I lead
  tu mènes — you (*s.*) lead
  il, elle mène — he, she leads
  nous menons — we lead
  vous menez — you (*pl.*) lead
  ils, elles mènent — they lead

usage *n.m.* — use, usage, wear

riche *adj.* — rich, wealthy

amitié *n.f.* — friendship, friendliness

immense *adj.* — huge, immense

créer — to create
  je crée — I create
  tu crées — you (*s.*) create
  il, elle crée — he, she creates
  nous créons — we create
  vous créez — you (*pl.*) create
  ils, elles créent — they create

titre *n.m.* — title

cri *n.m.* — cry, shout

combien *adv.* — how much, how many

verre *n.m.* — glass

complet (*m.*), complète (*f.*) *adj.* — complete, full up

village *n.m.* — village

compagnie *n.f.* — company

retour *n.m.* — return, reversal

mademoiselle *n.f.* (*pl.* mesdemoiselles) — miss

convenir — to suit, admit, fit (conjugated like venir)

page *n.f.* — page

chaud *adj.* — hot

gagner — to earn, gain, win

    je gagne I win   nous gagnons we win

    tu gagnes you (*s.*) win   vous gagnez you (*pl.*) win

    il, elle gagne he, she wins   ils, elles gagnent they win

allemand *adj.* — German

aspect *n.m.* — sight, aspect

supposer — to suppose, assume (conjugated like poser)

parent (*m.*), parente (*f.*) *n.* — parent, relative

ailleurs *conj.* — elsewhere

raconter — to tell, narrate (conjugated like conter)

voiture *n.f.* — car, cart, van

matière *n.f.* — matter, material

plaire — to please

    je plais I please   nous plaisons we please

    tu plais you (*s.*) please   vous plaisez you (*pl.*) please

    il, elle plaît he, she pleases   ils, elles plaisent they please

papier *n.m.* — paper

plupart *n.f.* — majority, greater part, most of

métier *n.m.* — trade, profession

adresser — to address (s'adresser ici, apply here)

membre *n.m.* — member

troisième *adj.* — third

hasard *n.m.*	chance, luck, accident
battre	to beat
je bats I beat	nous battons we beat
tu bats you (*s.*) beat	vous battez you (*pl.*) beat
il, elle bat he, she beats	ils, elles battent they beat
or *conj.*	now, but, well
théâtre *n.m*	theatre, drama
foi *n.f.*	faith
oser	to dare (conjugated like poser)
jardin *n.m.*	garden
brillant *adj.*	brilliant
ouvert *adj.*	open
autorité *n.f.*	authority
prêter	to lend, attribute
je prête I lend	nous prêtons we lend
tu prêtes you (*s.*) lend	vous prêtez you (*pl.*) lend
il, elle prête he, she lends	ils, elles prêtent they lend
volonté *n.f.*	will
or *n.m.*	gold
choisir	to choose
je choisis I choose	nous choisissons we choose
tu choisis you (*s.*) choose	vous choisissez you (*pl.*) choose
il, elle choisit he, she chooses	ils, elles choisissent they choose
merveilleux (*m.*), merveilleuse (*f.*) *adj.*	marvellous, wonderful
placer	to set, place
je place I set	nous plaçons we set
tu places you (*s.*) set	vous placez you (*pl.*) set
il, elle place he, she sets	ils, elles placent they set
attitude *n.f.*	behaviour, attitude
genre *n.m.*	genre, kind, manner
système *n.m.*	system

proposer	to propose (conjugated like poser)
événement *n.m.*	event, incident
derrière *prep.*	behind
marche *n.f.*	step, walking (en marche, in motion)
bientôt *adv.*	soon (à bientôt! so long!)
réussir	to result, succeed
je réussis I succeed	nous réussissons we succeed
tu réussis you (*s.*) succeed	vous réussissez you (*pl.*) succeed
il, elle réussit he, she succeeds	ils, elles réussissent they succeed
méthode *n.f.*	method
capable *adj.*	capable
avenir *n.m.*	future
marquer	to mark, score, show
je marque I mark	nous marquons we mark
tu marques you (*s.*) mark	vous marquez you (*pl.*) mark
il, elle marque he, she marks	ils, elles marquent they mark
défendre	to defend (conjugated like prendre)
exactement *adv.*	exactly
cheval *n.m.* (*pl.* chevaux)	horse
prétendre	to claim, assert (conjugated like prendre)
but *n.m.*	object, aim, goal
précis *adj.*	exact, accurate
maintenir	to maintain (conjugated like tenir)
passé *n.m.*	past
élément *n.m.*	element

également *adv.* — equally, likewise
comme *conj.* — as, seeing that
faux (*m.*), fausse (*f.*) *adj.* — false
relever — to raise, hold up (conjugated like lever)

tour *n.m.* — trip, tour, turn
réaliser — to realise, carry out
naturellement *adv.* — of course, naturally
froid *adj.* — cold
traverser — to cross, pass through
bleu *adj.* — blue
marché *n.m.* — market, deal
importer — to matter, be important (conjugated like porter)

désirer — to desire, wish
voie *n.f.* — way, track
auprès *adv.* — close to
accorder — to grant, agreed to
  j'accorde   I grant   nous accordons   we grant
  tu accordes   you (*s.*) grant   vous accordez   you (*pl.*) grant
  il, elle accorde   he, she grants   ils, elles accordent   they grant
économique *adj.* — economic
arbre *n.m.* — tree
américain — American

courant *n.m.*	current, stream
faible *adj.*	feeble, weak
concerner	to concern
actuel (*m.*), actuelle (*f.*) *adj.*	present, current
pierre *n.f.*	stone
davantage *adv.*	more
nu *adj.*	naked, bare
souhaiter	to wish

    je souhaite — I wish   nous souhaitons — we wish
    tu souhaites — you (*s.*) wish   vous souhaitez — you (*pl.*) wish
    il, elle souhaite — he, she wishes   ils, elles souhaitent — they wish

pluie *n.f.*	rain
ramener	to bring back (conjugated like mener)

défaut *n.m.*	lack, default, problem
cacher	to hide
prêt *adj.*	ready, prepared
chanter	to sing

    je chante — I sing   nous chantons — we sing
    tu chantes — you (*s.*) sing   vous chantez — you (*pl.*) sing
    il, elle chante — he, she sings   ils, elles chantent — they sing

conscience *n.m.*	conscience, consciousness
lourd *adj.*	heavy, dull
émotion *n.f.*	emotion
prononcer	to pronounce
aussitôt *adv.*	immediately
étoile *n.f.*	star

comporter — to comprise, require, call for (conjugated like porter)

rare *adj.* — rare

tuer — to kill
- je tue — I kill — nous tuons — we kill
- tu tues — you (*s.*) kill — vous tuez — you (*pl.*) kill
- il, elle tue — he, she kills — ils, elles tuent — they kill

soldat *n.m.* — soldier

propos *n.m.* — subject, purpose

craindre — to fear
- je crains — I fear — nous craignons — we fear
- tu crains — you (*s.*) fear — vous craignez — you (*pl.*) fear
- il, elle craint — he, she fears — ils, elles craignent — they fear

partout *adv.* — everywhere

fer *n.m.* — iron

terme *n.m.* — term, end

social *adj.* (*pl.* sociaux) — social

sang *n.m.* — blood

boire — to drink
- je bois — I drink — nous buvons — we drink
- tu bois — you (*s.*) drink — vous buvez — you (*pl.*) drink
- il, elle boit — he, she drinks — ils, elles boivent — they drink

joli *adj.* — pretty

terminer — to end, bring to an end
- je termine — I end — nous terminons — we end
- tu termines — you (*s.*) end — vous terminez — you (*pl.*) end
- il, elle termine — he, she ends — ils, elles terminent — they end

poète (*m.*), femme poète *or* poétesse (*f.*) *n.* — poet

fin *adj.* — fine

été *n.m.* — summer

ressembler — to resemble

charmant *adj.* — charming

droit *adj.*	right
devoir *n.m.*	duty, exercise (homework)
activité *n.f.*	activity
souvenir	to remember, recall (conjugated like venir)
aventure *n.f.*	adventure
connaissance *n.f.*	knowledge, acquaintance
public *n.m.*	public, people
intéressant *adj.*	interesting
avouer	to confess, acknowledge, admit
j'avoue I confess	nous avouons we confess
tu avoues you (*s.*) confess	vous avouez you (*pl.*) confess
il, elle avoue he, she confesses	ils, elles avouent they confess
justice n.f.	justice
bruit *n.m.*	noise, rumour
souci *n.m.*	care, worry
crise *n.f.*	crisis, attack (of nerves, etc.)
nord *n.m.*	north
complètement *adv.*	completely, entirely, totally, full
espoir *n.m.*	hope
abandonner	to abandon (conjugated like donner)
lit *n.m.*	bed
énorme *adj.*	huge, enormous
supporter	to support, endure (conjugated like porter)

beauté *n.f.* — beauty

passage *n.m.* — passage, crossing, flow

faveur *n.f.* — favour

pris *adj.* — occupied, busy

neige *n.f.* — snow

parvenir — to reach, arrive at (conjugated like venir)

quelquefois *adv.* — sometimes

centre *n.m.* — centre, center, middle

moral *adj.* (*pl.*moraux) — moral

employer — to employ

fameux (*m.*), fameuse (*f.*) *adj.* — famous

parfaitement *adv.* — perfectly

secret *n.m.* — secret

fournir — to supply
- je fournis   I supply
- tu fournis   you (*s.*) supply
- il, elle fournit   he, she supplies
- nous fournissons   we supply
- vous fournissez   you (*pl.*) supply
- ils, elles fournissent   they supply

contenir — to contain (conjugated like tenir)

ouvrier (*m.*), ouvrière (*f.*) *n.* — worker

figurer — to represent, imagine, figure
- je figure   I represent
- tu figures   you (*s.*) represent
- il, elle figure   he, she represents
- nous figurons   we represent
- vous figurez   you (*pl.*) represent
- ils, elles figurent   they represent

tableau *n.m.* (*pl.* tableaux) — board, painting, table

bas *adv.*	low down
militaire *adj.*	military
docteur *n.m.*	doctor
changement *n.m.*	change
diriger	to direct, control, run
je dirige I direct	nous dirigeons we direct
tu diriges you (*s.*) direct	vous dirigez you (*pl.*) direct
il, elle dirige he, she directs	ils, elles dirigent they direct
vaste *adj.*	vast
camarade *m. & n.f.*	comrade
national *adj.*	national
certes *adv.*	certainly, to be sure
circonstance *n.f.*	circumstance, event
fenêtre *n.f.*	window
fermé	closed
jeunesse *n.f.*	youth
mort *adj.*	dead
oh! *interj.*	oh!
pénétrer	to penetrate
je pénètre I penetrate	nous pénétrons we penetrate
tu pénètres you (*s.*) penetrate	vous pénétrez you (*pl.*) penetrate
il, elle pénètre he, she penetrates	ils, elles pénètrent they penetrate
sol *n.m.*	ground, earth
cependant *adv.*	meanwhile
intérieur *adj.*	inner, internal
mari *n.m.*	husband
particulièrement *adv.*	particularly

visite *n.f.*	visit
ton *n.m.*	tone, breeding, manners
commerce *n.m.*	commerce, trade
éviter	to avoid
j'évite I avoid	nous évitons we avoid
tu évites you (*s.*) avoid	vous évitez you (*pl.*) avoid
il, elle évite he, she avoids	ils, elles évitent they avoid
froid *n.m.*	cold
présent *adj.*	present
bouche *n.f.*	mouth
cependant *conj.*	yet, nonetheless, however
moderne *adj.*	modern
professeur *n.m.*	professor, teacher
conversation *n.f.*	conversation
après-midi *n.m.*	afternoon
égard *n.m.*	regard, respect
utile *adj.*	useful
droite *n.f.*	right-hand
maladie *n.f.*	illness, disease
trait *n.m.*	flash, stroke
bien *n.m.*	possession, good (biens, goods)
unique *adj.*	only, sole
réfléchir	to reflect, ponder

soi *pron.* — oneself, himself, herself, itself
principal *adj. (pl.* principaux) — principal, main
chance *n.f.* — chance, luck
président *n.m.* — president
crime *n.m.* — crime
prochain *adj.* — next, nearest
conclure — to conclude
  je conclus   I conclude
  tu conclus   you (*s.*) conclude
  il, elle conclut he, she concludes
  nous concluons we conclude
  vous concluez you (*pl.*) conclude
  ils, elles concluent they conclude
montagne *n.f.* — mountain
net (*m.*), nette (*f.*) *adj.* — clean, clearcut
opinion *n.f.* — opinion
sec (*m.*), sèche (*f.*) *adj.* — dry
fermer — to close
  je ferme   I close
  tu fermes   ou (*s.*) close
  il, elle ferme   he, she closes
  nous fermons   we close
  vous fermez   you (*pl.*) close
  ils, elles ferment   they close
rêve *n.m.* — dream
patron (*m.*), patronne (*f.*) *n.* — patron, master, employer
épreuve *n.f.* — proof, test
nul (*m.*), nulle (*f.*) *adj.* — non-existent, no

dehors *adv.*	outside
coin *n.m.*	corner, nook
étendre	to stretch, enlarge (conjugated like prendre)
témoin *n.m.*	witness
habiter	to inhabit, live in
magnifique *adj.*	magnificent
vin *n.m.*	wine
triste *adj.*	sad
crier	to shout, cry

je crie — I shout	nous crions — we shout
tu cries — you (*s.*) shout	vous criez — you (*pl.*) shout
il, elle crie — he, she shouts	ils, elles crient — they shout

foule *n.f.*	crowd, crush
absolument *adv.*	absolutely
réel (*m.*), réelle (*f.*) *adj.*	real
ouvrage *n.m.*	work, product
éprouver	to prove, test (conjugated like prouver, trouver)
excellent *adj.*	excellent
subir	to suffer, undergo

je subis — I suffer	nous subissons — we suffer
tu subis — you (*s.*) suffer	vous subissez — you (*pl.*) suffer
il, elle subit — he, she suffers	ils, elles subissent — they suffer

suivant *adj.*	next, following
campagne *n.f.*	plain, countryside, campaign
acheter	to buy

j'achète — I buy	nous achetons — we buy
tu achètes — you (*s.*) buy	vous achetez — you (*pl.*) buy
il, elle achète — he, she buys	ils, elles achètent — they buy

| ceci *pron.* | this |

soit *conj.*	whether, either
position *n.f.*	position
palais *n.m.*	palace, palate
accompagner	to accompany
lèvre *n.f.*	lip
durer	to last
juste *adj.*	just, right
salon *n.m.*	drawing-room, salon, saloon
remplacer	to replace (conjugated like placer)
terrain *n.m.*	ground, land
spectacle *n.m.*	spectacle, entertainment, show
étudier	to study (conjugated like crier)
ennemi *n.m.*	enemy
signaler	to report, mark
je signale I report	nous signalons we report
tu signales you (*s.*) report	vous signalez you (*pl.*) report
il, elle signale he, she reports	ils, elles signalent they report
désormais *adv.*	henceforth
prouver	to prove (conjugated like trouver)
repos *n.m.*	rest, repose
saison *n.f.*	season
reposer	to rest, replace (conjugated like poser)
plan *n.m.*	plan, drawing, plane

citer	to quote, cite, summon
précisément *adv.*	precisely
général *n.m.* (*pl.* généraux)	general
tôt *adv.*	soon
mariage *n.m.*	wedding, marriage
retirer	to retire, take back (conjugated like tirer)
fonction *n.f.*	function
preuve *n.f.*	evidence, proof
puissant *adj.*	powerful, strong
atmosphère *n.f.*	atmosphere
séparer	to separate
endroit *n.m.*	place, side
directeur (*m.*), directrice (*f.*) *n.*	director, directress
tromper	to deceive, betray (se tromper, to be mistaken)
envie *n.f.*	desire, envy
intérieur *n.m.*	interior (à l'intérieur, inside)
attirer	to attract, draw (conjugated like tirer)
sœur *n.f.*	sister

source *n.f.*	source, spring, origin
moitié *n.f.*	half
mémoire *n.f.*	memory, recollection
sauf *prep.*	save, except
sourire	to smile (conjugated like rire)
personnel (*m.*), personnelle (*f.*) *adj.*	personal
dépasser	to go beyond, overtake
soutenir	to support, sustain (conjugated like tenir)
personnage *n.m.*	personage, character
délicat *adj.*	sensitive, delicate
sauver	to save, preserve
passion *n.f.*	passion
apparence *n.f.* (N.B. spelling)	appearance
danger *n.m.*	danger
semblable *adj.*	like, similar
quant à *prep.*	with regard to
misère *n.f.*	misery
phénomène *n.m.*	phenomenon
autrement *adv.*	otherwise, differently

cheveu *n.m.* (*pl.* cheveux)	one hair, *pl.* the hair as a whole
inspirer	to inspire
santé *n.f.*	health
château *m.n.* (*pl.* châteaux)	castle, palace
province *n.f.*	province
mériter	to merit, deserve
surprise *n.f.*	surprise
vendre	to sell (conjugated like prendre)
avion *n.m.*	aeroplane, aircraft (par avion, by airmail)
premier (*m.*), première (*f.*) *n.*	first (occasion), première
fou (*m.*), folle (*f.*) *adj.*	mad, crazy
masse *n.f.*	mass
disposer	to dispose, lay out (conjugated like poser)
origine *n.f.*	origin, descent
appel *n.m.*	appeal, call
revoir	to see again, meet again (conjugated like voir)

formule *n.f.*	form, formula
prier	to beg, pray (je vous en prie! please do!) (conjugated like crier)
peau *n.f.* (*pl.* peaux)	skin, hide
malheureux (*m.*), malheureuse (*f.*) *adj.*	unhappy
développer	to stretch out, unroll, develop
désir *n.m.*	wish, desire
révolution *n.f.*	revolution
ensemble *n.m.*	whole, unity
quartier *n.m.*	district, quarter
sérieux (*m.*), sérieuse (*f.*) *adj.*	serious
avis *n.m.*	notice, advice, opinion
rapidement *adv.*	quickly
aider	to help, assist
prince *n.m.*	prince
front *n.m.*	forehead, front
billet *n.m.*	ticket, letter, bill
considérable *adj.*	considerable
anglais *adj.*	English, British
insister	to insist

aussi *conj.*	so, consequently
assister	to help (assister à, to attend, be present at)
tenter	to tempt, attempt
bateau *n.m.* (*pl.* bateaux)	boat
lendemain *n.m.*	day after, next day
fixer	to fix, assess
quelqu'un (*m.*), quelqu'une (*f.*) *pron.*	somebody, one (*pl.* quelques-un(e)s, a few)
million *n.m.*	million
livrer	to deliver, surrender
opération *n.f.*	operation
rapporter	to report, bring back, withdraw (conjugated like porter)
extérieur *adj.*	external, exterior
arrivée *n.f.*	arrival
regretter	to regret
indiquer	to indicate, lay down
arme *n.f.*	weapon
taire	to suppress, hush up (se taire, to be silent)
extraordinaire *adj.*	extraordinary
entretenir	to maintain, entertain (conjugated like tenir)

dent *n.f.*	tooth
commettre	to commit, risk (conjugated like mettre)
relation *n.f.*	relation, report
confier	to trust, entrust, confide
soudain *adv.*	suddenly
exiger	to require, call for, exact
installer	to install, equip
intention *n.f.*	intention
pleurer	to weep, mourn for
résoudre	to solve, resolve, settle
éclat *n.m.*	to clap, flash, splinter
pain *n.m.*	bread
illusion *n.f.*	illusion
remonter	to re-ascend, go up again (conjugated like monter)
défense *n.f.*	defence, prohibition
réduire	to reduce
solution *n.f.*	solution
étrange *adj.*	strange, odd
entraîner	to entail, carry along
brusquement *adv.*	abruptly

agent *n.m.*	agent
dit *adj.*	said, fixed, settled
éloigner	to remove, send away
mort *n.m.*	dead (person) (cf. la mort, death)
entourer	to encircle, surround
jadis *adv.*	formerly
attacher	to attach, bind
soirée *n.f.*	evening, reception, party
dimanche *n.m.*	Sunday
approcher	to approach
économie *n.f.*	economics, economy
gauche *n.f.*	left-hand side
production *n.f.*	production
déposer	to put down, deposit, depose (conjugated like poser)
printemps *n.m.*	Spring
tantôt *adv.*	soon, just now
lecture *n.f.*	reading
précédent *adj.*	preceding
perdu *adj.*	lost
texte *n.m.*	text

passé *adj.*	past
engager	to engage, start, involve, entangle
étage *n.m.*	storey, rank
avancer	to advance, put forward
mètre *n.m.*	metre, meter
entrée *n.f.*	entrance, admission
extrême *adj.*	extreme, utmost
fortune *n.f.*	fortune, luck
coucher	to put to bed (se coucher, to go to bed)
série *n.f.*	series, succession
affirmer	to assert, affirm
règle *n.f.*	rule
tort *n.m.*	error, wrong, injury
notion *n.f.*	notion, idea
asseoir	to set, pitch (s'asseoir, to sit down, conjugated below)

je m'assois (assieds)	nous nous assoyons
tu t'assois (assieds)	vous vous assoyez
il, elle s'assoit (assied)	ils, elles s'assoient

courage *n.m.*	courage
prévoir	to foresee, provide for (conjugated like voir, except future and conditional tenses)
vertu *n.f.*	valour, virtue, chastity
charger	to charge, load, burden
flamme *n.f.*	flame, passion

peintre *n.m.*	painter
frais (*m.*), fraîche (*f.*) *adj.*	fresh, cool
rêver	to dream, dream of
gare *n.f.*	station
explication *n.f.*	explanation
train *n.m.*	train, noise
admirable *adj.*	admirable
énergie *n.f.*	energy
forêt *n.f.*	forest
estimer	to estimate, esteem
médecin *n.m.*	(medical) doctor
français *n.m.*	Frenchman
imagination *n.f.*	imagination
précieux (*m.*), précieuse (*f.*) *adj.*	precious, affected
conséquence *n.f.*	consequence (par conséquent, en conséquence, consequently)
direction *n.f.*	conduct, management, direction
degré *n.m.*	step, degree, stage, percent proof
chargé *adj.*	loaded, charged

malade *m. & n.f.*	invalid, sick person
phrase *n.f.*	sentence, (musical) phrase
administration *n.f.*	administration, governing body, management
autrefois *adv.*	formerly, in the past
lait *n.m.*	milk
exercer	to exercise, practise (a trade)
officier *n.m.*	officer
réserve *n.f.*	reserve, reservation, hesitation
conception *n.f.*	conception, idea
avantage *n.m.*	advantage
port *n.m.*	port, carriage (of post, of a person)
expérience *n.f.*	experience, experiment
quart *n.m.*	quarter
sensible *adj.*	sensitive, perceptible
contact *n.m.*	contact
transformer	to transform
veille *n.f.*	staying up, watch, eve
tradition *n.f.*	tradition
sinon *conj.*	otherwise, if not
fête *n.f.*	festival, show

empire *n.m.* — authority, sway, empire
conseil *n.m.* — council, counsel, plan
terrible *adj.* — terrible
quantité *n.f.* — quantity
long *n.m.* — length
donné *adj.* — given
promener — to take for a walk (*but* je promène)
(se promener, go for a walk)

je promène I take a walk
tu promènes you (*s.*) take a walk
il, elle promène he, she takes a walk
nous promenons we take a walk
vous promenez you take a walk
ils, elles promènent they take a walk

hélas! *interj.* — alas!
revue *n.f.* — review, inspection, magazine
officiel (*m.*), officielle (*f.*) *adj.* — official
obliger — to force, compel, oblige
vide *adj.* — empty
toutefois *adv.* — nevertheless, yet, even so
humeur *n.f.* — humour, temper
concevoir — to conceive, understand
je conçois I conceive
tu conçois you (*s.*) conceive
il, elle conçoit he, she conceives
nous concevons we conceive
vous concevez you (*pl.*) conceive
ils, elles conçoivent they conceive
produit *n.m.* — product
certainement *adv.* — certainly
gloire *n.f.* — glory
portrait *n.m.* — portrait, face
banque *n.f.* — bank

génie *n.m.*	genius, engineering
promettre	to promise (conjugated like mettre)
vert *adj.*	green
progrès *n.m.*	progress
mise *n.f.*	setting, placing, bet
exposer	to exhibit, display, expose (conjugated like poser)
spécial *adj.*	special
victime *n.f.*	victim
poussière *n.f.*	dust
reprocher	to reproach, grudge
curiosité *n.f.*	curiosity
clef/clé *n.f.*	key
appartement *n.m.*	flat, apartment, room
malade *adj.*	sick, ill
nommer	to name
type *n.m.*	type, character, fellow
vitesse *n.f.*	speed
emporter	to carry, carry away (conjugated like porter)
international *adj.*	international
photographie *n.f.*	photograph, photography

céder	to give way, yield (*but* je cède)
je cède I give way	nous cédons we give way
tu cèdes you (*s.*) give way	vous cédez you (*pl.*) give way
il, elle cède he, she gives way	ils, elles cèdent they give way
oreille *n.f.*	ear
amant (*m.*), amante (*f.*) *n.*	lover
rapide *adj.*	rapid, swift
crédit *n.m.*	credit
deviner	to predict, guess
distance *n.f.*	distance
colonie *n.f.*	colony
race *n.f.*	race, breed, ancestry
partager	to share, divide
dos *n.m.*	back
élève *m. & n.f*	student, pupil
civilisation *n.f.*	civilisation
ombre *n.f.*	shade, shadow
noter	to note
influence *n.f.*	influence
physique *adj.*	physical
avance *n.f.*	lead, advance, projection
secret (*m.*), secrète (*f.*) *adj.*	secret

base *n.f.*	base, basis
marchand (*m.*), marchande (*f.*) *n.*	shopkeeper, tradesperson
matériel (*m.*), matérielle (*f.*) *adj.*	material, materialistic
réveiller	to awake, arouse (se réveiller, to wake oneself up)
célèbre *adj.*	famous, celebrated (*with* par, for)
mêler	to mingle, mix, shuffle
propriétaire *m. & n.f.*	proprietor, proprietress; landlord, landlady
retourner	to return, go back (conjugated like tourner)
prison *n.f.*	imprisonment, prison
doigt *n.m.*	finger
angoisse *n.f.*	anguish, distress
risquer	to risk
digne *adj.*	worthy, deserving (*with* de, of)
proposition *n.f.*	proposal, proposition
nouvelle(s) *n.f.*	piece of news, (news)
définitif (*m.*), définitive (*f.*) *adj.*	permanent, definitive
publier	to publish
bête *n.f.*	beast, blockhead

interroger	to examine, interrogate
statue *n.f.*	statue
animal *n.m.* (*pl.* animaux)	animal
outre *adv.*	further (en outre, besides)
film *n.m.*	film
organiser	to organise
rencontre *n.f.*	encounter, meeting, occasion
manifester	to show, evince, manifest
richesse *n.f.*	wealth
sacré *adj.*	holy, sacred
style *n.m.*	style
population *n.f.*	population
cour *n.f.*	court, courtyard
connu *adj.*	well-known, acquainted
intelligence *n.f.*	understanding, intelligence
troupe *n.f.*	troupe, throng, herd, troop
immédiatement *adv.*	immediately
chapitre *n.m.*	chapter, item
obligé *adj.*	compelled, indispensable, grateful

achever
　j'achève　I complete
　tu achèves　you (*s.*) complete
　il, elle achève　he, she completes
to complete, conclude (*but* j'achève)
　nous achevons　we complete
　vous achevez　you (*pl.*) complete
　ils, elles achèvent　they complete

langage　*n.m.*
language, speech

arracher
to snatch, pull away, tear out

intime　*m. & n.f.*
intimate friend

contenter
to gratify, satisfy (conjugated like tenter)

nécessité　*n.f.*
necessity

arrière　*adv.*
behind, backwards (*more usually* en arrière)

préférer
　je préfère　I prefer
　tu préfères　you (*s.*) prefer
　il, elle préfère　he, she prefers
to prefer (*but* je préfère)
　nous préférons　we prefer
　vous préférez　you (*pl.*) prefer
　ils, elles préfèrent　they prefer

éclater
to burst, flash, splinter

chair　*n.f.*
flesh, pulp

lentement　*adv.*
slowly

chasse　*n.f.*
hunt, hunting

sonner
to strike, sound, ring

date　*n.f.*
date (in time; *the fruit is* la datte)

leçon　*n.f.*
lesson

réunir
to convene, reunite (conjugated like unir)

tranquille　*adj.*
calm

chapeau　*n.m.* (*pl.* chapeaux)
hat

responsabilité　*n.f.*
responsibility

profiter
to take advantage (*with* de, of)

dépit *n.m.*	spite, resentment (en dépit de, in spite of)
cabinet *n.m.*	office, small room, cabinet
hésiter	to hesitate, falter
horreur *n.f.*	horror
précision *n.f.*	precision, accuracy
fier (*m.*), fière (*f.*) *adj.*	proud
accomplir	to accomplish, carry out
épaule *n.f.*	shoulder
manteau *n.m.* (*pl.* manteaux)	cloak, coat
introduire	to introduce (conjugated like produire)
observation *n.f.*	observation
réellement *adv.*	really, actually
serrer	to shake, clasp, put away
équilibre *n.m.*	balance, stability
résister	to resist, withstand
normal *adj.* (*pl.* normaux)	normal, standard
consister	to consist
larme *n.f.*	tear (en larmes, in tears)
dégager	to disengage, release, redeem
voisin *adj.*	neighbouring, next door, neighbor

neuf (*m.*), neuve (*f.*) *adj.*	new
sud *n.m.*	south
admirer	to admire
conclusion *n.f.*	conclusion
drame *n.m.*	drama, play
universel (*m.*), universelle (*f.*) *adj.*	universal
tâche *n.f.*	task
commander	to command, order, control
placé *adj.*	placed
évident *adj.*	obvious
malheur *n.m.*	accident, misfortune
police *n.f.*	police, policy
cesse *n.f.*	ceasing (sans cesse, unceasingly)
rechercher	to search for, enquire into (conjugated like chercher)
total *adj.*	total
fleuve *n.m.*	river
récent *adj.*	recent
presse *n.f.*	press, pressure
inviter	to invite

poids *n.m.*	weight
honte *n.f.*	shame
écarter	to brush aside, separate, dismiss
couvert *adj.*	covered
jaune *adj.*	yellow
désordre *n.m.*	disorder
discussion *n.f.*	discussion, argument
privé *adj.*	private
île *n.f.*	island
déterminer	to decide, determine
vague *adj.*	vague, dim
surpris *adj.*	surprised
impôt *n.m.*	tax
bloc *n.m.*	bloc, block
poule *n.f.*	hen
douleur *n.f*	pain, sorrow
lancer	to throw, launch, start
note *n.f.*	note, mark
appuyer	to support, press
lune *n.f.*	moon

entendu *adj.*	understood
menace *n.f.*	menace, threat
étranger (*m.*), étrangère (*f.*) *n.*	foreigner, stranger
réclamer	to complain, claim
cadre *n.m.*	frame, framework, cadre
branche *n.f.*	branch
organisation *n.f.*	organisation
solide *adj.*	solid
scientifique *adj.*	scientific
appliquer	to apply
création *n.f.*	creation
absence *n.f.*	absence
balle *n.f.*	ball, bullet
afin de *prep.*	in order to
capitaine *n.m.*	captain
enlever	to carry off, away (*but* j'enlève)

j'enlève to carry off   nous enlevons   we carry off
tu enlèves you (*s.*) carry off   vous enlevez   you (*pl.*) carry off
il, elle enlève he, she carries off   ils, elles enlèvent   they carry off

application *n.f.*	application
fixe *adj.*	fixed
juge *n.m.*	judge, magistrate, umpire

rayon *n.m.*	ray, radius, spoke
opposer	to oppose (conjugated like poser)
remercier	to thank
dangereux (*m.*), dangereuse (*f.*) *adj.*	dangerous
mesurer	to measure
parisien (*m.*), parisienne (*f.*) *adj.*	Parisian
respirer	to breathe
manœuvre *n.f.*	manœuvre, drill, driving
industrie *n.f.*	industry
séjour *n.m.*	stay, abode
individu *n.m.*	individual (person)
financier (*m.*), financière (*f.*) *adj.*	financial
indispensable *adj.*	indispensable
modeste *adj.*	modest
consacrer	to consecrate, devote
ressource *n.f.*	resource
fini *adj.*	finished

lors (= alors) *adv.*	when (lors de son arrivée, when he arrived)
intervenir	to intervene, interfere (conjugated like venir)
fruit *n.m.*	fruit
lecteur (*m.*), lectrice (*f.*) *n.*	reader
dresser	to make out, set out, prepare
violent *adj.*	violent
désigner	to design
midi *n.m.*	midday, south (après midi, afternoon)
résistance *n.f.*	resistance
quelconque *adj.*	any
dîner *n.m.*	dinner
naissance *n.f.*	birth
ressentir	to resent, feel (conjugated like sentir)
fidèle *adj.*	faithful
évoquer	to evoke
remplir	to fill, complete
provoquer	to provoke, cause
motif *n.m.*	motive, reason
mérite *n.m.*	merit, worth

recommencer	to start again (conjugated like commencer)
pitié *n.f.*	pity
chiffre *n.m.*	figure, amount, code
heureusement *adv.*	happily
aide *n.f.*	aid, rescue, relief (*m. & n.f.*, helper)
grandeur *n.f.*	size, greatness, splendour
propriété *n.f.*	property, ownership
atelier *n.m.*	studio, workshop
exception *n.f.*	exception
venu *adj.*	come
sucre *n.m.*	sugar
promenade *n.f.*	walk, walking, stroll
aborder	to land, berth, accost (conjugated like border)
culture *n.f.*	culture
justement *adv.*	properly, precisely
vers *n.m.*	verse, line
russe *adj.*	Russian
dessous *adv.*	beneath, below
garde *n.m.*	guard, care, watchman
carrière *n.f.*	career, racecourse
suprême *adj.*	supreme

station *n.f.*	station
actuellement *adv.*	at the present time
enfance *n.f.*	childhood
glisser	to slide, slip
mystérieux (*m.*) mystérieuse (*f.*) *adj.*	mysterious
herbe *n.f.*	grass, herb
réflexion *n.f.*	reflection, thought
exact *adj.*	exact, true, punctual
peinture *n.f.*	paint, painting
soumettre	to submit, subject (conjugated like mettre)
pont *n.m.*	bridge
absolu *adj.*	absolute
territoirre *n.m.*	territory
demeure *n.f.*	residence, home, house
industriel (*m.*) industrielle (*f.*) *adj.*	industrial
seigneur *n.m.*	lord, nobleman
colère *n.f.*	anger
favorable *adj.*	favourable
choix *n.m.*	choice

dominer	to rule, dominate, overcome
langue *n.f.*	tongue, language
proche *adj.*	near
fil *n.m.*	thread, wire, edge
inventer	to invent
sommeil *n.m.*	sleep, sleepiness
union *n.f.*	union, unity
couvrir	to cover (conjugated like ouvrir)
historique *adj.*	historic, historical
accident *n.m.*	accident
instinct *n.m.*	instinct

régler — to rule, regulate (*but* je régle)

    je règle — I rule   nous réglons — we rule
    tu règles — you (*s.*) rule   vous réglez — you (*pl.*) rule
    il, elle règle — he, she rules   ils, elles règlent — they rule

charge *n.f.*	burden, office, expense
association *n.f.*	association
excès *n.m.*	excess
vis-à-vis *prep.*	with regard to
folie *n.f.*	madness
possession *n.f.*	possession
critique *n.f.*	criticism, review
satisfaire	to satisfy (conjugated like faire)

tendre *adj.*	tender, soft
interdire	to forbid, disconcert (conjugated like dire)
cinéma *n.m.*	cinema, films
définir	to define (conjugated like finir)
casse *n.f.*	fund, cash, case, hold-up
combat *n.m.*	fight, contest
pièce *n.f.*	piece, room, play
fantaisie *n.f.*	fancy, imagination, fantasy
religeux (*m.*), religeuse (*f.*) adj.	religious
voeu n.m. (*pl.* voeux)	vow, wish
hommage *n.m.*	tribute, homage
aboutir	to succeed, lead to, result in
paysage *n.m.*	landscape
lampe *n.f.*	light, lamp
plaindre	to pity (se plaindre, to complain)
décret *n.m.*	decree
chaise *n.f.*	chair
gauche *adj.*	left, clumsy

ranger	to arrange, tidy away (conjugated like manger)
tendance *n.f.*	tendency, trend
vain *adj.*	vain
monument *n.m.*	monument
littérature *n.f.*	literature
course *n.f.*	race, running, excursion
incapable *adj.*	incapable, inefficient
retard *n.m.*	delay (en retard, late)
entreprise *n.f.*	business, undertaking
dehors *n.m.*	exterior, outside
mince *adj.*	slender, thin
construire	to construct, build, assemble
respect *n.m.*	respect, regard
cercle *n.m.*	circle
tour *n.f.*	tower
revanche *n.f.*	revenge (en revanche, on the other hand)
choc *n.m.*	impact, clash, shock
pénible *adj.*	laborious, painful
soulever	to raise, arouse (conjugate like lever; je soulève)

   je soulève   I raise   nous soulevons   we raise
   tu soulèves   you (*s.*) raise   vous soulevez   you (*pl.*) raise
   il, elle soulève he, she raises   ils, elles soulèvent   they raise

réaction *n.f.*	reaction

poche *n.f.*	pocket, bag
dîner	to dine
obscur *adj.*	dark, obscure, humble
vrai *n.m.*	truth, right
foyer *n.m.*	hearth, fire, focus
élevé *adj.*	exalted, high, lofty
machine *n.f.*	engine, machine
document *n.m.*	document
sombre *adj.*	dim, gloomy
affreux (*m.*), affreuse (*f.*) *adj.*	hideous, frightful
rejoindre	to catch up, reunite (conjugated like joindre)
mystère *n.m.*	mystery
épais (*m.*), épaisse (*f.*) adj.	thick
tendresse *n.f.*	tenderness
nouveau *n.m.*	item of news (du nouveau, something new)
gaz *n.m.*	gas
inquiétude *n.f.*	unease, anxiety
secours *n.m.*	help, assistance
précaution *n.f.*	precaution

épouser	to marry
modèle *n.m.*	pattern, model
lent *adj.*	slow
idéal *n.m.* (*pl.* idéals or idéaux)	ideal
renseignement *n.m.*	an item of information (usually *pl.* des renseignements, some information)
établi *adj.*	established
comédie *n.f.*	comedy, play
considéré *adj.*	considered, respected
décembre *n.m.*	December
pardonner	to pardon (conjugated like donner)
risque *n.m.*	risk
roman *n.m.*	novel
rire *n.m.*	laughter
durée *n.f.*	wear, duration
tache *n.f.*	stain, blemish
démontrer	to demonstrate (conjugated like montrer)
abri *n.m.*	shelter
consommation *n.f.*	consumption, drink, expenditure
boîte *n.f.*	box, night-club
direct *adj.*	direct, straight

constant *adj.*	constant
trou *n.m.*	hole
prière *n.f.*	prayer, request
croix *n.f.*	cross
couper	to cut
agréable *adj.*	agreeable
régulier (*m.*), régulière (*f.*) *adj.*	regular
feuille *n.f.*	leaf, sheet
arranger	to arrange (s'arranger, to manage)
consacré *adj.*	consecrated, established
déliceux (*m.*), délicieuse (*f.*) *adj.*	delicious
jambe *n.f.*	leg
transport *n.m.*	transport
kilomètre *n.m.*	kilometre, kilometer
relatif (*m.*), relative (*f.*) *adj.*	relative
lien *n.m.*	tie, bond
rond *adj.*	round
déclaration *n.f.*	declaration
crainte *n.f.*	fear
surprendre	to surprise (conjugated like prendre)

sommet *n.m.*	summit
singulier (*m.*), singulière (*f.*) *adj.*	singular
transformation *n.f.*	transformation
client (*m.*), cliente (*f.*) *n.*	client
août *n.m.*	August
café *n.m.*	coffee, coffee-house
décor *n.m.*	decoration, décor
préparation *n.f.*	preparation
ça *adv.*	hither (ça et là , here and there)
limite *n.f.*	boundary, limit
escalier *n.m.*	stairs, staircase
varié *adj.*	varied
pratique *n.f.*	practice, application
plante *n.f.*	plant, sole of the foot
écrivain *n.m.*	writer, author
particulier (*m.*), particulière (*f.*) *n.*	private person, individual
danser	to dance
sympathie *n.f.*	sympathy, attraction
république *n.f.*	republic
rapprocher	to draw near, bring together (conjugated like approcher)

traité *n.m.*	treaty, treatise
finance *n.f.*	finance
volontiers *adv.*	willingly
dessin *n.m.*	drawing, design
sauter	to jump, change, explode
talent *n.m.*	talent
double *adj.*	double
possibilité *n.f.*	possibility
nez *n.m.*	nose
programme *n.m.*	programme (UK), program (US), show, broadcast (radio)
essai *n.m.*	trial, test, essay
religion *n.f.*	religion, faith
establishment *n.m.*	establishment
lutte *n.f.*	struggle, wrestling
navire *n.m.*	ship
échange *n.m.*	exchange
patte *n.f.*	foot (of bird), paw (of animal)
miracle *n.m.*	miracle
boulevard *n.m.*	boulevard, rampart
proportion *n.f.*	proportion

coûter	to cost
brouillard *n.m.*	mist
éloigné *adj.*	far off, remote
hauteur *n.f.*	height, arrogance
député *n.m.*	deputy, delegate
emploi *n.m.*	use, employment
haine *n.f.*	hatred
opérer	to operate, perform (*but* j'opère)
j'opère I operate	nous opérons we operate
tu opères you (*s.*) operate	vous opérez you (*pl.*) operate
il, elle opère he, she operates	ils, elles opèrent they operate
triomphe *n.m.*	triumph
accuser	to accuse, show, own up to
évolution *n.f.*	evolution
soigner	to tend, look after
nettement *adv.*	clearly, cleanly
numéro *n.m.*	number
bref (*m.*), brève (*f.*) *adj.*	brief, short
interrompre	to interrupt (conjugated like rompre)
régiment *n.m.*	regiment
généralement *adv.*	generally
couple *n.m.*	couple, pair
sort *n.m.*	destiny, chance, spell

téléphoner	to telephone
spirituel (*m.*), spirituelle (*f.*) *adj.*	spiritual
reprise *n.f.*	resumption, recapture, stage in sport (round, bout, second half)
intelligent *adj.*	intelligent
représentant (*m.*), représentante (*f.*) *n.*	representative
heurter	to knock, run into
morceau *n.m.* (*pl.* morceaux)	bit, piece, morsel of food
nullement *adv.*	not at all, by no means
septembre *n.m.*	September
exceptionnel (*m.*), exceptionnelle (*f.*) *adj.*	exceptional
pratique *adj.*	practical
musée *n.m.*	museum
humanité *n.f.*	humanity, human nature
jouir	to enjoy
repousser	to reject, recoil, repel (conjugated like pousser)
classique *adj.*	classical
rejeter	to reject, throw back, cast up (conjugated like jeter)
juste *adv.*	rightly, exactly
allusion *n.f.*	allusion

fonds *n.m.*	fund, funds, means
anglais (*m.*), anglaise (*f.*) *n.*	English person
cou *n.m.*	neck
profit *n.m.*	profit, benefit
commercial *adj.* (*pl.* commerciaux)	commercial
secrétaire *m.& n.f.*	secretary
ferme *adj.*	firm, steady
discuter	to discuss, argue
collection *n.f.*	collection
amuser	to amuse, entertain
vigueur *n.f.*	vigour (UK), vigor (US) (en vigueur, in force)
prétexte *n.m.*	pretext
indépendant *adj.* (N.B. spelling)	independent
bénéfice *n.m.*	profit, benefit
trésor *n.m.*	treasure
parfum *n.m.*	perfume
démarche *n.f.*	step, gait
vide *n.m.*	void, vacuum, empty space
terrasse *n.f.*	terrace, pavement (outside a café)

rideau *n.m.* (*pl.* rideaux)	curtain
cité *n.f.*	city
facilement *adv.*	easily
aile *n.f.*	wing
résumer	to summarize
goutte *n.m.*	drop, sip
entièrement *adv.*	entirely
calme *adj.*	calm
carte *n.f.*	map, card, sheet of paper
utiliser	to use
enthousiasme *n.m.*	enthusiasm
content *adj.*	satisfied, pleased
frontière *n.f.*	frontier, border, boundary
écrit *adj.*	written
visiter	to visit
professionnel (*m.*), professionnelle (*f.*) *adj.*	professional
rose *n.f.*	rose
obéir	to obey

prévenir	to anticipate, avert, inform (conjugated like venir)
parcourir	to travel through, skim (conjugated like courir)
chasseur (*m.*), chasseuse (*f.*) *n.*	hunter, huntress
recouvrir	to recover, cover (conjugated like couvrir)
ange *n.m.*	angel
fonctionnaire *n.m.*	official, civil servant
chasser	to hunt, chase, drive away
correspondre	to correspond
fusil *n.m.*	gun
préciser	to state, specify
pointe *n.f.*	point, peak
divin *adj.*	divine
costume *n.m.*	costume
troubler	to trouble, confuse, muddy
laine *n.f.*	wool
presser	to press, squeeze, hurry on
cuisine *n.f.*	cooking, kitchen
gré *n.m.*	liking, will
dû (*m.*), due (*f.*) *adj.*	due, owing
essentiel (*m.*), essentielle (*f.*) *adj.*	essential

harmonie *n.f.*	harmony, agreement
proclamer	to proclaim
durant *prep.*	during
univers *n.m.*	universe
dommage *n.m.*	damage (Quel dommage! What a pity!)
conférence *n.f.*	conference, lecture
petit (*m.*), petite (*f.*) *n.*	child, young (of an animal)
consentir	to consent (conjugated like sentir)
faiblesse *n.f.*	weakness, failing
situé *adj.*	situated
accent *n.m.*	accent, tone
poste *n.m.*	post, station (*not* sense of 'mail')
notamment *adv.*	notably
sacrifier	to sacrifice
examen *n.m.*	examination
peser	to weigh (*but* je pèse)

je pèse   I weigh   nous pesons   we weigh
tu pèses   you (*s.*) weigh   vous pesez   you (*pl.*) weigh
il, elle pèse   he, she weighs   ils, elles pèsent   they weigh

bain *n.m.*	bath
maîtresse *n.f.*	mistress
cadavre *n.m.*	corpse, carcase
princesse *n.f.*	princess

nerveux (*m.*), nerveuse (*f.*) *adj.*	nervous
argument *n.m.*	argument, summary
rude *adj.*	uncouth, rough, harsh
écrier	to cry out (conjugated like crier)
retraite *n.f.*	retirement, retreat
occupé *adj.*	to occupy, employ, inhabit
entretien *n.m.*	upkeep, maintenance, interview
congrès *n.m.*	congress
décisif (*m.*), décisive (*f.*) *adj.*	decisive
fièvre *n.f.*	fever
fatigué *adj.*	tired
surveiller	to supervise, look after (conjugated like veiller)
excuser	to excuse (someone) (s'excuser, to excuse oneself)
instruction *n.f.*	lesson, training
précéder	to precede (conjugated like céder, i.e. je précède)
victoire *n.f.*	victory
réservé *adj.*	reserved, shy
adopter	to adopt
exercice *nm.*	exercise

allonger	to lengthen
destinée *n.f.*	destiny
debout *adv.*	upright
né *adj.*	born
bande *n.f.*	band, strip, flock
procurer	to obtain
dépense *n.f.*	expense, dispensary
confirmer	to confirm
huile *n.f.*	oil
briser	to break, smash
surface *n.f.*	surface
faim *n.f.*	hunger
choisi *adj.*	chosen
personnalité *n.f.*	personality
bataille *n.f.*	battle
voyageur (*m.*), voyageuse (*f.*) *n.*	traveller
édifice *n.m.*	building
signifier	to mean
philosophie *n.f.*	philosophy

œuf *n.m.*	egg
nourrir	to nourish, rear, maintain
médiocre *adj.*	mediocre
exécuter	to perform, execute
toit *n.m.*	roof
tellement *adv.*	so
regret *n.m.*	regret
dépendre	to depend, belong to (conjugated like prendre)
mensonge *n.m.*	lie
catégorie *n.f.*	category
éclairer	to light, instruct
confondre	to confuse, baffle
pressé *adj.*	crowded, hurried
comte *n.m.*	count (French), earl (English)
répandre	to pour out, spread, scatter
construction *n.f.*	building, construction
éternel (*m.*), éternelle (*f.*) *adj.*	eternal
gêner	to inconvenience, obstruct
continu *adj.*	continuous
mission *n.f.*	mission

réserver	to reserve
brusque *adj.*	abrupt, sudden
capital *n.m.* (*pl.* capitaux)	capital (money)
majorité	majority
organisme *n.m.*	organism
épargner	to save, be sparing
rigueur *n.f.*	rigour, severity (de rigueur, obligatory)
attaque *n.f.*	attack
magasin *n.m.*	shop, warehouse
pencher	to lean, incline
incident *n.m.*	incident
user	to use
département *n.m.*	department, ministry
royal *adj.*	royal
représentation *n.f.*	representation, performance, exhibition
humide *adj.*	humid, damp
transporter	to transport, transfer (conjugated like porter)
reproche *n.m.*	reproach
ouest *n.m.*	west
destin *n.m.*	destiny

tissu *n.m.*	material, texture
suffisant *adj.*	sufficient
colonne *n.f.*	column, pillar
coupé *adj.*	cut (up), broken
goûter	to taste, enjoy
mécanique *adj.*	mechanical
maman *n.f.*	mummy
fatigue *n.f.*	fatigue
charbon *n.m.*	coal, carbon
apprécier	to value, estimate, appreciate
souffle *n.m.*	breath
charme *n.m.*	charm
emmener	to lead away, take away (*but* j'emmène)

  j'emmène   I lead away
  tu emmènes you (*s.*) lead away
  il, elle emmène he, she leads away

  nous emmenons   we lead away
  vous emmenez   you (*pl.*) lead away
  ils, elles emmènent   they lead away

coutume *n.f.*	custom, habit
bassin *n.m.*	basin, dock, bowl
isolé *adj.*	isolated
fuir	to flee, avoid
complexe *adj.*	complex
souffrance *n.f.*	suffering, suspense
forcer	to force

douceur *n.f.*	gentleness, sweetness
composé	composite, compound
génération *n.f.*	generation
boue *n.f.*	mud, dirt
éteindre	to put out, switch off (conjugated like teindre)
conseiller	to counsel, recommend
liaison *n.f.*	liaison
lointain *adj.*	distant
sou *n.m.*	(colloquially) penny (je suis sans le sou, I am broke)
régner	to reign
permanent *adj.*	permanent
enseignement *n.m.*	teaching, tuition
exposition *n.f.*	exhibition, statement
saluer	to greet
perte *n.f.*	loss, destruction
extrêmement *adv.*	extremely
infini *adj.*	infinite
convention *n.f.*	convention
honnête *adj.*	honest, decent
probable *adj.*	probable

confus *adj.*	confused
rendez-vous *n.m.*	appointment, meeting-place
vente *n.f.*	sale
juillet *n.m.*	July
obligation *n.f.*	obligation, bond
douloureux (*m.*), douloureuse (*f.*) *adj.*	sad, painful
témoigner	to bear, witness, prove
conduite *n.f.*	conduct, direction, driving
moteur *n.m.*	motor, engine
variété *n.f.*	variety
sûrement *adv.*	surely, safely
quai *n.m.*	quay, embankment, platform
delà *adv.*	beyond
quoique *conj.*	though, although
consulter	to consult
quotidien (*m.*), quotidienne (*f.*) *adj.*	daily
contrôle *n.m.*	checkpoint, inspection, test
actif (*m.*), active (*f.*) *adj.*	active

savant (*m.*), savante (*f.*) *n.*	scholar, scientist
inférieur *adj.*	lower, inferior
toilette *n.f.*	toilet, washing and dressing
tâcher	to strive, try
bleu *n.*	blue
uniquement *adv.*	solely, simply
fixé adj.	fixed
perfection *n.f.*	perfection
mentir	to lie
réjouir	to delight, entertain (conjugated like jouir)
plat *n.m.*	dish, course, flat (of racing, tires)
courant *adj.*	current, flowing, running
déjeuner *n.m.*	lunch, breakfast
contribuer	to contribute
probablement *adv.*	probably
assis *adj.*	seated
profondément *adv.*	deeply, profoundly
décision *n.f.*	decision
plage *n.f.*	beach, sea resort

noble *adj.*	noble
trace *n.f.*	track, trace
chat (*m.*), chatte (*f.*) *n.*	cat
éveiller	to wake up (conjugated like veiller)
diable *n.m.*	devil
populaire *adj.*	popular
conquérir	to conquer
réunion *n.f.*	assembly, reunion
tragique *adj.*	tragic
débarrasser	to clear, rid
endormir	to put to sleep, bore (s'endormir, to fall asleep)
remarquable *adj.*	remarkable
étendu *adj.*	extended, outstretched
niveau *n.m.* (*pl.* niveaux)	level
formation *n.f.*	education, formation
merveille *n.f.*	wonder
violence *n.f.*	violence
chute *n.f.*	fall
néanmoins *conj.*	yet, nevertheless
profondeur *n.f.*	depth

jurer	to swear
souffler	to breathe, pant, blow
drôle *adj.*	funny, odd
merci *n.m.*	thanks
sac *n.m.*	bag, sack
tapis *n.m.*	carpet, cover
brun *adj.*	brown
modification *n.f.*	modification
infiniment *adv.*	infinitely
température *n.f.*	temperature
chauffeur (*m.*), chauffeuse (*f.*) *n.*	driver, stoker
inscription *n.f.*	inscription
traduire	to translate, summon, indict
savant *adj.*	erudite, skilful
acquérir	to acquire, obtain (*but* j'acquiers)
j'acquiers I acquire	nous acquérons we acquire
tu acquiers you (*s.*) acquire	vous acquérez you (*pl.*) acquire
il, elle acquiert he, she acquires	ils, elles acquièrent they acquire
volume *n.m.*	volume
concert *n.m.*	concert, agreement
légitime *adj.*	legitimate
comparer	to compare
assemblée *n.f.*	assembly

miroir *n.m.*	mirror
chant *n.m.*	song, singing
janvier *n.m.*	January
horrible *adj.*	horrible
modifier	to modify
manque *n.m.*	lack, shortage
armé *adj.*	armed, equipped
mépris *n.m.*	contempt
tombe *n.f.*	tomb
prolonger	to prolong, extend
unité *n.f.*	unit, unity
allumer	to light, inflame
commission *n.f.*	commission, errand
nier	to deny
épuiser	to exhaust, sell out
rivière *n.f.*	river
lutter	to fight, struggle
lac *n.m.*	lake
débattre	to debate, discuss (conjugated like battre)
éclairé *adj.*	lit, well-informed

écraser	to crush, squash, overwhelm
plainte *n.f.*	complaint, groan, legal action
évidence *n.f.*	evidence, obviousness
protéger	to protect (*but* je protège)
toile *n.f.*	cloth, linen, oil painting
alcool *n.m.*	alcohol
commencement *n.m.*	beginning
sagesse *n.f.*	wisdom
communiquer	to communicate, infect
architecte *n.m.*	architect
indifférent *adj.*	indifferent, insensible, immaterial
horizon *n.m.*	horizon
transmettre	to transmit (conjugated like mettre)
justifier	to justify
réputation *n.f.*	reputation
subtil *adj.*	subtle, delicate, shrewd
réalisé *adj.*	realised, carried out
chanson *n.f.*	song
sacrifice *n.m.*	sacrifice
samedi *n.m.*	Saturday

longuement *adv.*	slowly, for a long time
allemand *n.m.*	German
posé	calm, grave, steady
espace *n.m.*	space, distance
intimité *n.f.*	intimacy, depths
accueillir	to receive, greet (conjugated like cueillir)
primitif (*m.*), primitive (*f.*) *adj.*	primitive, primary
académie *n.f.*	academy
genou *n.m.* (*pl.* genoux)	knee
original *adj.* (*pl.* originaux)	original
recommander	to recommend, register (conjugated like commander)
contrat *n.m.*	contract, agreement
récit *n.m.*	story, account
blanc *n.m.*	white
directement *adv.*	directly
tristesse *n.f.*	sadness
échec *n.m.*	check, setback
adversaire *n.m.*	opponent
délivrer	to deliver

audace *n.f.*	audacity, boldness
trouble *n.m.*	disturbance, trouble
inspecteur (*m.*), inspectrice (*f.*) *n.*	inspector
vérifier	to check, confirm, verify

je vérifie   I check
tu vérifies   you (*s.*)check
il, elle vérifie   he, she checks

nous vérifions   we check
vous vérifiez   you (*pl.*) check
ils, elles vérifient   they check

distinction *n.f.*	distinction
forcé *adj.*	forced,
orgueil *n.m.*	pride
parc *n.m.*	park
orient *n.m.*	Orient
résolution *n.f.*	resolution
calme *n.m.*	calm(ness)
immédiat *adj.*	immediate
viande *n.f.*	meat,
italien (*m.*), italienne (*f.*) *adj.*	Italian
accrocher	to hook, hang

j'accroche   i hang
tu accroches you (*s.*) hang
il, elle accroche   he, she hangs

nous accrochons   we hang
vous accrochez   you(*pl.*) hang
ils, elles accrochent   they hang

colline *n.f.*	hill
fumer	to smoke

je fume   i smoke
tu fumes   you(*s.*) smoke
il, elle fume he, she, smokes

nous fumons   we smoke
vous fumez   you (*pl.*) smoke
ils, elles fument   they smoke

ardent *adj.*	burning, passionate, fierce

autant 19
auteur 23
automobile 31
autorité 36
autour 18
autre 5, 7
autrefois 57
autrement 49
aux 2
avance 60
avant 10, 28
avantage 57
avec 3
avenir 37
aventure 41
avion 50
avis 51
avoir 1
avouer 41

bain 86
balle 68
bande 88
banque 58
bas 29, 43
base 61
bassin 91
bataille 88
bateau/x 52
battre 36
beau/x 7
beaucoup 8
beauté 42
bel/le 7
bénéfice 83
besoin 14
bête 61
bien 3, 44
bientôt 37
billet 51
blanc/he 15, 99
bleu 38, 94
bloc 67
boire 40
bois 32

boîte 77
bon/ne 6
bonheur 31
bord 26
bouche 44
boue 92
boulevard 80
bout 21
branche 68
bras 25
br-ef, -ève 81
brillant 36
briser 88
brouillard 81
bruit 41
brun 96
brusque 90
brusquement 53
bureau/x 31
but 37

ça 5, 79
cabinet 65
cacher 39
cadavre 86
cadre 68
café 79
caisse 74
calme 84, 100
camarade 43
campagne 46
capable 37
capitaine 68
capit-al , -aux 90
car 8
caractère 19
carrière 71
carte 84
cas 12
catégorie 89
cause 13
ce/t/te 1, 2
ceci 46
céder 60
cela 5

célèbre 61
celle/s 6
celui 6
centre 42
cependant 43, 44
cercle 75
certain 7
certainement 58
certes 43
ces 1
cesse 66
cesser 26
ceux 6
chacun 18
chair 63
chaise 74
chambre 15
champ 28
chance 45
changement 43
changer 21
chanson 98
chant 97
chanter 39
chapeau/x 63
chapitre 62
chaque 8
charbon 91
charge 73
chargé 56
charger 55
charmant 40
charme 91
chasse 63
chasser 85
chass-eur, -euse 85
chat/te 95
château/x 50
chaud 35
chauff-eur, -euse 96
chef 28
chemin 23
ch-er, -ère 16
chercher 9
chev-al, -aux 37
cheveu/x, 50
chez 7

montrer 11
monument 75
mor-al, -aux 42
morceau/x 82
mort 18, 43, 54
mot 10
moteur 93
motif 70
mourir 19
mouvement 14
moyen 17
mur 30
musée 82
musique 34
mystère 76
mystéri-eux, -euse 72

naissance 70
naître 33
nation-al, -aux 43
nature 19
naturel/le 28
naturellement 38
navire 80
ne 1
né 88
néanmoins 95
nécessaire 26
nécessité 63
neìge 42
nerv-eux, -euse 87
net/te 45
nettement 81
n-euf, -euve 66
nez 80
ni 8
nier 97
niveau/x 95
noble 95
noir 20
nom 11
nombre 18
nombr-eux, -euse 23
nommer 59
non 5

nord 41
norm-al, -aux 65
nos 4
notamment 86
note 67
noter 60
notion 55
notre 4
nôtre 64
nourrir 89
nouveau/x 8, 76
nouvel/le/s 8, 61
nu 39
nuit 12
nul/le 45
nullement 82
numéro 81

obéir 84
objet 23
obligation 93
obligé 62
obliger 58
obscur 76
observation 65
observer 27
obtenir 21
occasion 33
occupé 87
occuper 23
odeur 64
oeil 8
oeuf 89
oeuvre 17
officiel/le 58
officier 57
offrir 16
oh! 43
oiseau/x 32
ombre 60
on 2
opération 52
opérer 81
opinion 45
opposer 69

or 36
ordre 19
oreille 60
organisation 68
organiser 62
organisme 90
orgueil 100
orient 100
origin-al, -aux 99
origine 50
oser 36
ou 3
où 3
oublier 16
ouest 90
oui 15
outre 62
ouvert 36
ouvrage 46
ouvr-ier, -ière 42
ouvrir 16

page 35
pain 53
paix 22
palais 47
papier 35
par 2
paraître 8
par avion 50
parc 100
parce que 9
parcourir 85
pardonner 77
pareil 25
parent 35
parfait 27
parfaitement 42
parfois 16
parfum 83
parisien/ne 69
parler 6
parmi 17
parole 22
part 11

many, too 7
march 33
mark 37, 47, 67
market 38
marriage 48
marry 77
marvellous 36
mass 50
master 17, 45
material 35, 61, 91
materialistic 61
matter 35, 38
me 3, 6
mean 13, 88
means 17, 83
meanwhile 43
measure 15, 69
meat 100
mechanical 91
mediocre 89
meet 16
meeting 62
meeting place 93
member 35
memento 19
memory 19, 49
menace 68
men and women 13
merely 9
merit 50, 70
method 37
metre 55
midday 70
middle 23
mild 28
military 43
milk 57
million 52
mingle 61
minister 30
ministry 64, 90
minute 23
miracle 80
mirror 97
misery 49
misfortune 66
miss 35
mission 89

mist 81
Mister (Mr) 4
mistress (Mrs) 11, 86
mix 61
model 77
modern 44
modest 69
modification 96
modify 97
moment 8, 21
money 21
month 12
monument 75
moon 67
moral 42
more 2, 39
morning 12
morsel 82
mother 20
motion, in 37
motive 70
motor 93
mountain 45
mourn for 53
mouth 44
movement 14, 30
much 8
much, how 34
much, not 25
much, so 5, 9
much, too 25
mud 92
muddy 85
mummy 91
museum 82
music 34
my 3
mysterious 72
mystery 76

naked 39
name 11, 59
nap 29
narrate 35
narrow 64
nation 19

national 43
natural 28
naturally 38
nature 19
near 11, 73
nearest 45
nearly 11
necessary 26
necessary, be 4
necessity 63
neck 83
need 14, 26
neighbouring 65
neither 8
nervous 87
never 6
nevertheless 16, 44, 58, 95
new 8, 66, 76
news 61, 76
newspaper 25
next 10, 45, 46, 65
nice 6
night 12
night-club 77
no 5, 45
noble 95
nobleman 72
noise 41, 56
non-existent 45
nook 46
no one 9, 24
nor 8
normal 65
north 41
nose 80
not 1, 2, 5
notably 86
not at all 18, 82
note 27, 60, 67
nothing 5
notice 51
notion 55
nourish 89
novel 77
now 10, 36
number 18, 81
numerous 23

understood 68
undertaking 75
unease 76
unhappy 51
union 73
unit 97
unity 51, 73, 97
universal 66
universe 86
unknown 64
unroll 51
until 7
up 27
upkeep 87
upon 2
upper 33
upright 88
up to 7
usage 34
use 34, 81, 84, 90
useful 44
useless 28
usually 28
utmost 55

vacate 18
vacuum 83
vague 67
vain 75
valour 55
value 15, 21, 91
van 35
varied 79
variety 93
various 26
vast 43
verify 100
verse 71
very 4, 17
victim 59
victory 87
view 15
vigour 83
village 34
violence 95
violent 70

virtue 55
visit 44, 84
voice 19
void 83
volume 96
vow 74

wait for 12
wake 61
wake up 95
walk 71
walk, go for 58
walk, take for 58
walking 37, 71
wall 30
want 5, 14
war 9
warehouse 90
warfare 9
washing 94
watch 27, 57
watchman 71
water 13
way 12, 18, 21, 23, 38
weak 39
weakness 86
wealth 62
weapon 52
wear 34, 77
weather 5
wedding 48
week 21
weep 53
weigh 86
weight 67
well 3, 36
well-informed 97
well-known 62
west 90
what 7, 12
when 5, 11, 70
where 3
whereas 27
whether 47
which 1, 2, 7, 17
while 27

white 15, 99
who 2, 17
whole 51
whole, on the 19
whom 1, 17
why 15
wide 33
wife 7
will 36, 85
willingly 80
win 35
wind 30
window 43
wine 46
wing 84
winter 30
wire 73
wisdom 98
wish 5, 38, 39, 51, 74
wit 13
with 3, 7
withdraw 52
without 4
withstand 65
witness 46
witness, bear 93
woman 7
wonder 95
wood 32
wool 85
word 10, 22
work 17, 22, 46
worker 42
works 33
workshop 71
world 8, 12
worry 41
worth 15, 70
worth, be 24
worthy 61
wrestling 80
write 15
writer 79
writing-desk 31
written 84
wrong 55